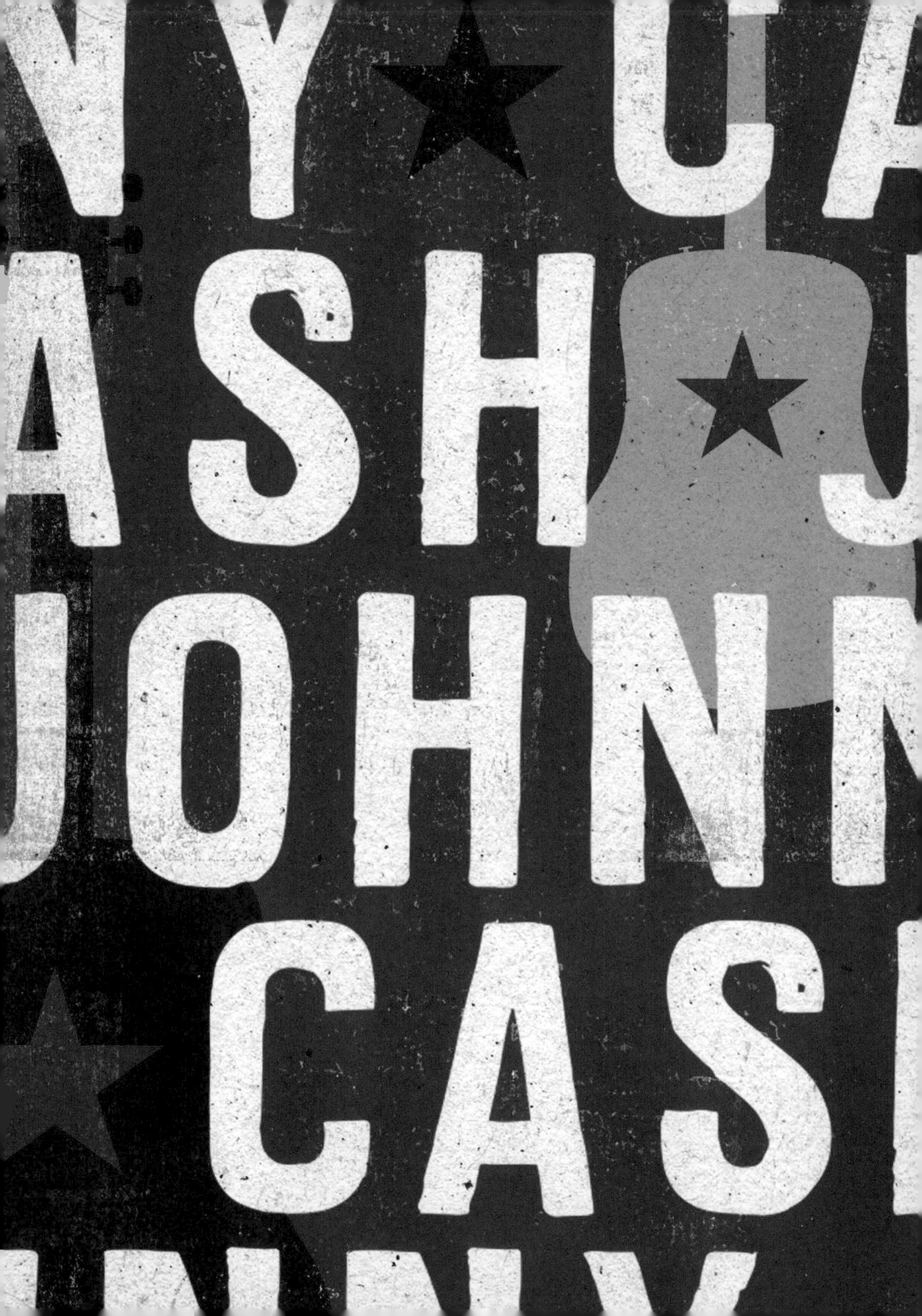

NY CA
ASH J
JOHN
CAS

TO:

FROM:

DATE:

WALKING THE LINE

90 DEVOTIONS OF TRUTH & HOPE BASED ON THE FAITH OF JOHNNY CASH

LIVE YOUR FAITH

CONTENTS

CHOOSE LOVE 1

All your life, you will be faced with a choice. You can choose love or hate. . . . I choose love.

—Johnny Cash

Three things will last forever—faith, hope, and love—and the greatest of these is love.

—I Corinthians 13:13 nlt

I choose love: three words that can change the world. One person at a time. One encounter at a time.

Jesus showed us what the words look like in action. He chose love, always—often in the most unexpected of ways. And usually in stark contrast to the people around Him.

Case in point: the people of Jericho, who chose the subtlest kind of hatred toward a blind beggar in their midst. They ignored the man. No doubt many of them also grumbled to one another about the problem of panhandling on their roadsides. When the blind man dared to make his presence known, they tried to silence and hide him. Jesus made the more difficult choice in responding to the man. He gave him His full attention. He showed him kindness. He asked about the man's need and then committed to doing something about it. Jesus chose love and changed a life forever.

Case in point: the religious leaders of Jesus' day, who chose outraged hatred toward a woman they caught having an adulterous affair. They dragged the woman to Jesus to publicly humiliate her and then threatened to do worse. Jesus refused to join their shame parade. He ignored the label of "adulteress" that the hypocritical lynch mob used to try to pigeonhole and condemn the woman. Instead, Jesus chose to see her for who she was, and not just for what she'd done. He reminded her accusers that their moral high ground wasn't as high—or as moral—as they thought it was. Jesus stood by the woman, unconcerned about how His own reputation might suffer. And after her accusers drifted away one by one, He offered the woman a word of encouragement and motivation, instead of condemning her. Jesus chose love and changed a life forever.

Case in point: Peter, who chose self-hatred after he failed Jesus miserably on the night of His arrest. Peter wept bitter tears after his failure. But when the two men met again after Jesus' resurrection, Jesus chose a loving reconciliation. He didn't criticize or accuse Peter. He didn't play on Peter's guilt. Instead, Jesus reminded Peter of his worth. He spoke to him like a beloved friend. He entrusted him with a sacred responsibility. Jesus chose love and changed a life forever.

What does it look like for someone who isn't the Son of God to choose love? It looks like a kind response to someone who insulted you on social media. It looks like a well-timed, heartfelt compliment for someone who's struggling with confidence. It looks like a quiet vigil at the side of someone who's grieving. It looks like an invitation to someone who doesn't often get included. It looks like a blanket, shoes, or a meal delivered to a homeless person.

Each choice we make to show love to others makes a difference. Every time we say "I choose love," through our words and actions, we help turn the tide of hate. We change the world by changing lives—one person at a time, one encounter at a time.

HEAVENLY FATHER, THANK YOU FOR CHOOSING TO LOVE ME. PLEASE GIVE ME THE WISDOM TO RECOGNIZE WHAT LOVE LOOKS LIKE IN A GIVEN SITUATION AND THE COURAGE TO CHOOSE IT. IN JESUS' NAME. AMEN.

THE SPARRING PARTNER WITHIN

Sometimes I am two people. Johnny is the nice one.
Cash causes all the trouble. They fight.
—JOHNNY CASH

For I have the desire to do what is good, but I cannot carry it out.
For I do not do the good I want to do, but the evil I do not want to
do—this I keep on doing. Now if I do what I do not want to do, it
is no longer I who do it, but it is sin living in me that does it.
—ROMANS 7:18–20 NIV

Johnny Cash used his first and last names for the wholesome and trouble-some sides of his dual nature. The apostle Paul just called his good and evil. Whatever names we use, all of us can empathize with the struggle.

What happens to our good intentions when circumstances go bad? Why is the last thing we could ever imagine saying often the first thing out of our mouths? Why are some temptations so irresistible? Why does our troublesome nature seem to know every vulnerable spot of our wholesome nature when the two battle?

These personal battles take up more of our time and energy than many of us would care to admit. But God sees every one of them. He knows our hearts. He knows our sincere desire to defeat the negative, destructive urges that seem to have us in their grip. He sees the obstacles that keep us from enjoying the life He intends for us.

In His Word, He makes it clear that the most effective battle plan for win-ning the War of Self is (1) to equip our good nature and (2) cut the supply line to our evil nature. God is the key to the first strategy. His Holy Spirit lives inside every believer, giving our "Johnny" nature the spiritual and emotional reinforcements we need for battle. We couldn't ask for a more powerful ally. The Spirit speaks to us through our conscience, guiding our steps and warning us when our "Cash" nature starts to rear its head.

God invites us to pray when the battle seems inevitable. He uses the words and stories of the Bible to inspire us. He gives us confidence and assures us that victory is possible.

As for the second strategy, we cut the supply line to our evil nature by recognizing its triggers and the things that give it strength. We identify the people, places, and circumstances that make us vulnerable to temptation and take steps to avoid them. We surround ourselves with people who root for the "Johnny" side of our nature.

We celebrate our victories by giving God all the credit. But we don't allow ourselves to get complacent. We remind ourselves that our "Cash" nature is constantly lurking, waiting for us to lower our guard. We stay sharp by staying close to God, His Word, and His people.

We mark our defeats, first, by asking God's forgiveness for our failure. We learn what we can from the battle and move on. We don't dwell on our losses. We don't allow our failures to define us. Instead, we prepare for the next battle, with God's help.

And then we turn our gaze outward. We recognize that everyone in our orbit is waging similar battles within. We become allies of their "Johnny" nature. And we extend to them the grace, patience, understanding, and encouragement they need.

> **HEAVENLY FATHER, YOU KNOW MY STRUGGLE. THANK YOU FOR MAKING VICTORY POSSIBLE OVER THE DARK SIDE OF MY NATURE. PLEASE GIVE ME THE STRENGTH AND WILL TO FIGHT EACH BATTLE AS IT COMES. IN JESUS' NAME. AMEN.**

REBEL WITH A CAUSE

I wore black because I liked it. I still do, and wearing it still means something to me. It's still my symbol of rebellion—against a stagnant status quo, against our hypocritical houses of God, against people whose minds are closed to others' ideas.

—Johnny Cash

"Speak up for the people who have no voice, for the rights of all the misfits! Speak out for justice! Stand up for the poor and destitute!"

—Proverbs 31:8–9 The Message

Johnny Cash understood that conformity robs us of one of our most precious gifts: our platform. That goes for conformity in music, in life, and in the Christian faith. Conformity limits our potential.

Johnny Cash left a powerful legacy because he used his platform to shine a light on injustice and hypocrisy. He spoke unpopular truths on behalf of those who had no voice. He sang for the misfits and the forgotten in our culture. He was unapologetic about his relationship with God and his reliance on God's leading.

Like Jesus, he challenged the status quo. And he encouraged others to do the same. He wore black as a reminder—to himself and to the world—that he marched to a different drummer and stood for something important.

Like Johnny Cash, each of us has a unique voice. Some voices are bold and confrontational. They command attention. Some voices are quietly effective. They reward careful listening. Some voices are laced with humor or hard-earned wisdom. Others cut straight to the heart of a matter with plainspoken directness. What's important is that our unique voice speaks to certain people in ways other voices can't.

Each of us has a unique perspective. Our one-of-a-kind blend of experiences, influences, personality traits, and God-given gifts causes us to view the world in a way no one else can. That unique vision is a gift from God, one that can be used powerfully to help others. Each of us has the ability to reach, influence, comfort, and encourage people whom others may not be able to reach as effectively.

Each of us has a unique opportunity to carve an important path through this world. We do that by not settling for the easy road. By not traveling the well-trampled ground that the majority prefer. By not taking directions from popular opinion. We carve a meaningful path by following God's lead. By going against the grain as often as necessary.

The journey can be lonely and difficult at times. Along the way, it helps to have reminders of our unique voice, platform, perspective, and opportunity. It may be a picture of a parent or grandparent who set an unforgettable example for us to follow. It may be a physical or emotional scar that we wear like a badge of honor because it represents our resilience and ability to overcome. It may be a verse, poem, lyric, or quote that speaks our truth. It may be a memento that symbolizes our strength and sense of purpose. Or, as with Johnny Cash, it may be a color or style that says to the world, "By God's grace, I will be a force to be reckoned with. I will not be content with the status quo. I will make a difference."

> DEAR GOD, THANK YOU FOR MAKING ME UNIQUE AND FOR GIVING ME A PLATFORM TO SPEAK YOUR TRUTH. HELP ME KEEP MY VOICE DISTINCT, SO THAT IT DOESN'T GET DROWNED OUT IN A CHORUS OF CONFORMITY. IN JESUS' NAME. AMEN.

THE IMPORTANT THINGS

The things that have always been important: to be a good man, to try to live my life the way God would have me, to turn it over to Him that His will might be worked in my life, to do my work without looking back, to give it all I've got, and to take pride in my work as an honest performer.

—JOHNNY CASH

The last and final word is this: Fear God. Do what He tells you. And that's it.

—ECCLESIASTES 12:13–14 THE MESSAGE

What is truly important?

There's no shortage of experts ready to answer that question for us. In fact, entire industries are devoted to it. Live your truth. Build your brand. Look your best. Invest wisely. Exercise. Eat well. Work hard. Play hard. Dream big.

Certainly no one would argue that it's important to be a good spouse. And a good parent. And a good son or daughter. And a good sibling. And a good friend. And a good worker. And a good neighbor. And a good citizen.

Each of us could probably add at least a dozen more truly important things to this list. And that creates a dilemma. With so many important things demanding our attention, how can we give them the emphasis they deserve?

Solomon, the writer of Ecclesiastes and one of the wisest men who ever lived, had the answer: *fear God and keep His commandments.* In everything we do.

To fear God is to give Him His deserving place in our lives. To put Him at the center of everything we do. To make His commandments our highest priority. When we do that, God blesses our efforts beyond our wildest dreams.

That's how we manage the important things in our lives: we aim to please God in each area. Period. When we make His will our priority, He manages the rest.

For example, we put God at the center of our parenting by introducing our kids to His Word. We show them what it looks like to love God and love others. We help them understand that discipline is a part of that love. We hold them to high standards but are quick to offer forgiveness and grace.

We put God at the center of our work by investing it with the integrity that Johnny Cash talked about. We use the gifts God has given us and give Him credit for them. We refuse to give less than our best effort. We put the needs of coworkers, clients, and customers ahead of our own. We go the extra mile. We make ourselves essential through the quality of our work and the spirit of service we bring to the job.

When we make honoring God our priority, we weave a thread of integrity through every important thing in our lives. We lessen the pull of unhealthy influences. We keep our competitive nature in check. We reduce the temptation to cut corners for success.

When we make honoring God our priority, we can strike the proper balance between pride and humility. We can look on with justifiable pride at the things God has accomplished through us. But by keeping Him first, we maintain the humility that is essential to our spiritual well-being.

> **HEAVENLY FATHER, I WANT TO PLEASE YOU AND DO YOUR WILL. THAT'S MY MOTIVATION. PLEASE HELP ME KEEP THAT FOCUS AND SHOW ME WAYS TO DO YOUR WILL IN EVERY AREA OF MY LIFE. IN JESUS' NAME. AMEN.**

IT'S A GIFT

My mother . . . said, "God has His hand on you . . . don't ever forget the gift."
. . . That's the first time she had called it the gift . . . and she referred to my
singing . . . writing . . . my voice . . . performing . . . any part of it, that's the
gift. . . . I guess it was to remind me I didn't deserve it, it was a gift . . . not so
much that I didn't deserve it, but it was something special that God gave me.

—JOHNNY CASH

God has given each of you a gift from His great variety of spiritual gifts.
Use them well to serve one another. Do you have the gift of speaking?
Then speak as though God Himself were speaking through you. Do you
have the gift of helping others? Do it with all the strength and energy that
God supplies. Then everything you do will bring glory to God through
Jesus Christ. All glory and power to Him forever and ever! Amen.

—I PETER 4:10–11 NLT

Johnny Cash's poignant memory of his mother resonates powerfully in two ways. First, it reminds us of our own God-given gifts. God created each of us with a specific set of skills and abilities. For instance, some people are naturally comfortable in leadership positions. They step up when others are looking for direction, inspiration, and motivation. They know how to get the most from others and how to get people to buy into a common vision or plan.

Some people are gifted at bringing order from chaos. They see the big picture and how things fit together within it. They create workable schedules. They maintain databases. They know how to organize, how to streamline, and how to increase efficiency. They make life more convenient for others.

Some people have the gift of emotional support. They are relational first responders. They fearlessly enter people's lives at critical times, often when others are too uncomfortable to help. They're unafraid of messy emotions. They know what to say and when to stay quiet. Their words of comfort go soul-deep.

Our job is to discover our gifts, recognize them for what they are, and put them to use.

Second, the story reminds us that it's important to recognize and encourage other people's God-given gifts. We can do for others what Johnny Cash's mother did for him. We can point out skills and abilities that other people may not know they have. Or we can point out the full extent of gifts that people might suspect they have.

The key is to observe, to pay attention to other people's strong points. When we see them, we can make them known through compliments and heartfelt encouragement.

We can give people ideas for making the most of their gifts. Some people know exactly what their gifts are but don't know how to put them to use. Or even where to begin. They could use creative input from someone who sees a bigger picture. If we ask God to give us the wisdom, perhaps we can be that person.

We can help people celebrate the One who gives all gifts. We, like Johnny Cash's mother, can help them appreciate the solemn but awesome responsibility that comes from being specially equipped by God.

FATHER, THANK YOU FOR THE GIFTS YOU HAVE GIVEN ME. HELP ME PUT MY GIFTS TO USE TO HELP OTHERS AND TO BRING YOU GLORY. THANK YOU FOR THE PEOPLE IN MY LIFE WHO RECOGNIZED MY GIFTS AND ENCOURAGED ME TO USE THEM. GUIDE ME IN DOING THE SAME FOR OTHERS. IN JESUS' NAME. AMEN.

SPHERES OF INFLUENCE

Well, they said about Jesus . . . He dines with publicans and sinners. . . . Paul said, "I will become all things to all men in order that I might win some for Christ now." . . . I don't have Paul's calling. . . . That's not my calling, to go out and become all things to all men to win them for Christ. . . . But sometimes I can be a signpost . . . sometimes I can sow seed. . . . And posthole diggers and seed sowers are pretty important in the building of the Kingdom.

—Johnny Cash

Make your light shine, so that others will see the good that you do and will praise your Father in heaven.

—Matthew 5:16 CEV

Our daily encounters may seem random from our perspective, the result of pure chance. From God's perspective, though, they're as tightly choreographed as a Broadway number. Each of us, at any given moment, has a sphere of influence—an area in which we can make our presence known. Sometimes our sphere is small and includes very few people; sometimes it's much larger and includes a crowd.

We enter each other's spheres in a given place, at a given time, for a reason. God gives us a chance, however brief, to shine His light in our own unique way.

Our spheres of influence change constantly, from sitting in the stands of a kid's ballgame to standing in line at the grocery to running through a neighborhood to meeting new clients at work.

Every time our sphere of influence changes, new opportunities present themselves. Opportunities to make Jesus known. Opportunities to show what it means to follow Him. Some people seize on these opportunities and verbally present the gospel as often as they can. The apostle Paul was big on this approach. Yet those of us who prefer a less bold and less direct strategy can still make an impact in our spheres of influence.

The key is to approach everything we do with integrity, kindness, and loving concern for others. When we make those priorities the core of who we are and how we approach daily life, they can't help but come out of us in an organic way, one that registers with other people.

Even the briefest interactions can be infused with this spirit. And, as Johnny Cash explained, they can serve as signposts that point the way to the One who makes our spirit possible. They can serve as seeds that we sow in people's lives, which can take root and begin to grow an interest in God.

Even the smallest gesture can sow seeds and perhaps eventually make a big impression. A show of sportsmanship during a game. An offer to help carry groceries. A listening ear for someone who needs one. Paying for the order of the next person in the drive-through lane. Buying an extra fast-food meal for a homeless person. As our spheres of influence change, so do our opportunities.

And if we keep our light shining, if we look for ways to serve as signposts and seed sowers, we may find that God expands our spheres of influence and gives us even more opportunities to serve Him and make a difference.

> FATHER, THANK YOU FOR THE OPPORTUNITIES YOU GIVE ME EVERY DAY TO MAKE A DIFFERENCE IN OTHER PEOPLE'S LIVES. HELP ME RECOGNIZE THAT EVERY TIME MY SPHERE OF INFLUENCE CHANGES, I HAVE A NEW OPPORTUNITY TO POINT THE WAY TO YOU OR SOW SEEDS THAT MAY TAKE ROOT IN SOMEONE'S LIFE. IN JESUS' NAME. AMEN.

ARGUING 7 WITH GOD

*I make no bones about where I stand . . . as a believer. . . . I'm a great man
of faith. . . . I don't think that there's a way to shake my faith in God. . . . I've
never doubted God, but I've argued. . . . And then I've realized what a puny
thing that is to argue with God. . . . It was a totally one-sided argument. . . .
I was really arguing with myself. . . . But my God is not a God of wrath.*

—JOHNNY CASH

*A man in the crowd answered. "Teacher, I brought You my son,
who is possessed by a spirit that has robbed him of speech. . . .
But if You can do anything, take pity on us and help us."
"'If You can'?" said Jesus. "Everything is possible for one who believes."
Immediately the boy's father exclaimed, "I do
believe; help me overcome my unbelief!"*

—MARK 9:17, 22–24 NIV

I n arguing with God, Johnny Cash followed in the footsteps of some of the
heroes of the faith. Abraham argued with God. The father of the nation of Israel haggled with the Almighty over the lives of the people of Sodom and Go-
morrah.

Moses argued with God at least twice. The man who led the Israelites out of
slavery in Egypt balked when God first called him, offering excuses as to why
he was the wrong person for the job. Later, he intervened when God threatened to destroy the Israelites for their disobedience.

Gideon argued with God. Like Moses, the general chosen to lead Israel
in battle didn't believe he was the right person for God's call. He needed to
be convinced.

Jonah argued with God. The Old Testament prophet resented God's calling for him to warn the people of Nineveh about God's impending judgment. Jonah didn't want the Ninevites, his enemies, to repent. He wanted them destroyed. So he balked at his assignment.

None of their arguments or objections had any real impact on God. They didn't change His mind or show Him the error of His ways, because there is no error in God's ways. Their counterpoints simply confirmed God's wisdom and affirmed His will. Chances are, some of the men came to the same conclusion that Johnny Cash did: that when we argue with God, we're really arguing with ourselves.

Like the desperate father who begged for Jesus' help, we're showing the limits of our belief and asking God to help us move past our unbelief.

God, in His mercy, recognizes that questioning—and even arguing—often leads to a stronger faith and a better understanding of our role in God's plan. We may not see ourselves as capable of fulfilling our role, but God does. And He's willing to help us see it, too, by countering our objections.

Likewise, we may not always understand the things God allows to happen in our lives. And in our pain, we may pose some pointed questions and accusations. God understands that too. He didn't strike down Abraham, Moses, Gideon, or Jonah for arguing with Him. And He won't punish us for expressing our sincere emotions. Instead, He helps us work through our pain and confusion, even if the process involves some blunt questions on our part.

> **HEAVENLY FATHER, THANK YOU FOR YOUR PATIENCE AND UNDERSTANDING WHEN I QUESTION YOU OR STRUGGLE TO UNDERSTAND YOUR WILL FOR MY LIFE. HELP MY UNBELIEF. STRENGTHEN MY TRUST IN YOU. GIVE ME THE WISDOM TO UNDERSTAND WHAT I CAN AND THE FAITH TO ACCEPT WHAT I CAN'T. IN JESUS' NAME. AMEN.**

MATTER OF THE HEART

He's a God that sees all and knows all and knows the hearts of men . . .
and knows my heart. . . . And He's the only One who does . . . 'cause He's
got the only mind that could understand such a complicated heart.

—JOHNNY CASH

But the LORD said to Samuel, "Don't judge by his appearance
or height, for I have rejected him. The LORD doesn't see
things the way you see them. People judge by outward
appearance, but the LORD looks at the heart."

—I SAMUEL 16:7 NLT

How can someone discover what we're truly like? Our words certainly offer some solid clues. The way we talk to people and the things we choose to talk about reveal quite a bit about our attitude, personality, background, and interests. But sometimes our words can be misleading. Lies, half-truths, sarcasm, and other verbal tricks can obscure the real person behind them.

The same goes for our actions. The way we carry ourselves, the activities and people we choose to involve ourselves with, the way we follow-through (or not) on the things we say all reveal key aspects of who we are. Yet actions can also be manipulated. We can live one way in public and another way in private. Skilled actors can make people believe just about anything.

In order to truly understand someone, we have to know the source of their motivation, the engine that drives everything they do. The Bible refers to it as our heart. It's the core of our being, the real person inside the words and actions. Nothing about our heart can be faked or hidden. As Johnny Cash points out, it's a complicated, messy place. And it's what God sees when He looks at us.

On the one hand, that can be a scary thought. The prospect of having our innermost thoughts, attitudes, and motivations laid bare before *anyone*, let alone our holy heavenly Father, is enough to make anyone uncomfortable. Yet God doesn't recoil from what He sees when He looks into the depths of our hearts. Nothing there is beyond His grace or forgiveness.

As if that weren't amazing enough, God's insistence on looking at our hearts also opens a world of possibilities to us, because He doesn't dwell on our limitations. Instead, He sees the full extent of our potential. The passage from I Samuel 16 above deals with the prophet Samuel's search for a king for Israel. No one—not even Samuel himself—imagined that a young shepherd could be the perfect candidate. But God looked past the shepherd exterior and saw a king's heart in David. And the heart was all that mattered.

What does God see when He looks past our exteriors? What potential does He see in us that would seem unimaginable to anyone else? Nothing we've ever done can disqualify us from the role God intends for us. If we invite Him to have His way in our hearts, to clean out what doesn't belong in them and fill them with what does, we can begin to align our own views of ourselves with God's view of us. We can begin to see the potential He sees in our hearts.

FATHER, NOTHING IS HIDDEN FROM YOUR SIGHT. YOU SEE MY INNER CORE. YOU KNOW WHAT'S IN MY HEART AND YOU LOVE ME, EVEN WHEN YOU DON'T LIKE WHAT YOU SEE. HELP ME RECOGNIZE THE POTENTIAL THAT YOU SEE IN ME. WORK IN MY HEART SO THAT I CAN BE THE PERSON YOU CREATED ME TO BE. IN JESUS' NAME. AMEN.

Just a closer walk with Thee,
Grant it, Jesus, is my plea,
Daily walking close to Thee,
Let it be, dear Lord, let it be.

—"Just a Closer Walk with Thee"
(author unknown)

YOU VISITED ME

When I was selling records, like '69, '70, and was making all these appearances and doing all these interviews . . . I'd made a public profession to faith as a Christian, and people were really confused . . . like, "How can you say you're a Christian and do that and do that and do that . . ." You know, "When you go to prison, you play for those killers and those rapists. . . . You cuddle prisoners. . . ." You don't cuddle prisoners. I go because I was told to go. . . . It's part of my . . . commission as a Christian to perform for those people . . . which was the reason I did it in the first place.

—JOHNNY CASH

"Then the King will say to the people on His right, 'Come, My Father has given you His blessing. Receive the kingdom God has prepared for you since the world was made. . . . I was in prison, and you visited Me.'
"Then the good people will answer, 'Lord, when did we see You . . . in prison and care for You?'
"Then the King will answer, 'I tell you the truth, anything you did for even the least of My people here, you also did for Me.'"

—MATTHEW 25:34, 36–37, 39–40 NCV

Jesus identifies so closely with hurting people, including those in prison, that He considers it a personal favor if we visit and care for them, and takes it as a personal rejection if we ignore them. Johnny Cash stepped far out of his comfort zone to perform for and minister to people in prison. How many lives did he change by going where few others dared?

If we hope to have an impact on Jesus and the people who have a special place in His heart, we have to be willing to step outside our comfort zones as well. Several local and national prison ministries do life-changing work with the incarcerated population. These vital outreach organizations would welcome our involvement.

And while these ministries are essential, we need to recognize that not all prisons have bars. Some prisons are of our own making. There are people who are imprisoned by guilt, something in their past that they can't forgive themselves for. There are people who are imprisoned by their reputation. They've resigned themselves to being what people say they are, because they can't seem to change popular opinion. There are people who are imprisoned by fear and anxiety. They're trapped by emotions they have no control over. There are people who are imprisoned by circumstances. Their location, culture, family, economic status, or other factors place extreme restrictions on them. There are people who are imprisoned by illness or disability. Their bodies can't enjoy the freedom of their minds, and vice versa.

These are the people Jesus points us to. They're the ones He identifies most closely with. They're the ones who give us a chance to do something for the Lord Himself. Johnny Cash had to convince nearly everyone around him that visiting the incarcerated was a vital ministry—and a commission he couldn't refuse. We need only to convince ourselves.

The call is irresistible: *Anything you do for the least of My people, you do for Me.*

FATHER, THANK YOU FOR CARING ABOUT EVERYONE, ESPECIALLY THOSE WHO GET OVERLOOKED IN OUR SOCIETY. THANK YOU FOR GIVING ME A CHANCE TO BE PART OF YOUR OUTREACH TO THEM. GIVE ME THE COURAGE TO MOVE OUT OF MY COMFORT ZONE AND CONNECT WITH IMPRISONED PEOPLE. IN JESUS' NAME. AMEN.

A FRIEND INDEED

You know . . . [I'm] slowly learning . . . what friendship is. . . . And it should be pretty simple 'cause the Bible says there's a friend that sticks closer than a brother . . . and greater love has no man . . . than would lay down his life for his friend. . . . I've had so many really good friends.

—JOHNNY CASH

There is no greater love than to lay down one's life for one's friends.

—JOHN 15:13 NLT

In the Gospel of John, Jesus sets a pretty high bar for loving others. And in His death on the cross, He set the standard for love and friendship. Jesus laid down His life for His friends—and for the entire world. So when we want to learn what friendship is, the best place to start is with the Son of God. That's who Johnny Cash had his eyes on when he wanted to learn.

Jesus spoke the truth to His friends, even when it made them uncomfortable. For instance, He didn't try to sugarcoat the harsh realities of what a friendship with Him would mean. He told His disciples what they would have to sacrifice if they wanted to follow Him. He warned them that they would face rejection, slander, suffering, and even death. Jesus risked losing friends by telling hard truths, but He gained the respect and trust of those who stayed by His side.

Jesus confronted His friends when they were wrong. Once, after Jesus predicted to His disciples that He would soon die, Peter—who was one of Jesus' closest earthly friends—had the nerve to take Him aside and tell Him that he (Peter) would never let it happen. Jesus immediately called Peter a stumbling block and pointed out the selfishness and egotism in his words.

Jesus recognized His friends' potential and helped them see it too. He took fishermen, a tax collector, and assorted blue-collar laborers and turned them into missionaries, church builders, and world changers.

Jesus comforted His friends when they were scared. Some of the Lord's miracles undoubtedly unsettled His disciples, especially the time He walked across the sea at night and climbed into their boat. What's more, they became enemies of some of the most powerful people in Israel just by being Jesus' followers. Through it all, Jesus was quick to reassure them, bolster their courage, and calm them with His presence.

Jesus forgave His friends when they messed up. Peter panicked on the night of Jesus' arrest and three times claimed not to know Him. Peter had trouble forgiving himself for his failure, but Jesus didn't. After His resurrection, He sought Peter out, offered forgiveness, and repaired the relationship.

Very few of us will be faced with the prospect of laying down our life for our friends. But there are other things we can sacrifice in order to strengthen the bonds of our friendships. We can lay down the pride that causes us to lash out when we're hurt. We can lay down the competitiveness and jealousy that keep us from sincerely celebrating our friends' accomplishments. We can lay down our comfort, our knee-jerk judgmental attitudes, our time, our energy, and our resources for the sake of our closest companions. That's what it means to be the kind of friend Jesus was—and the kind of friend He calls us to be.

> **HEAVENLY FATHER, THANK YOU FOR THE FRIENDS WHO HAVE MADE A DIFFERENCE IN MY LIFE. HELP ME BE THE KIND OF FRIEND WHO POINTS OTHERS TO YOU, WHO ENCOURAGES THEM TO REACH THEIR POTENTIAL AND WHO WILL SACRIFICE MY OWN WANTS AND NEEDS FOR THEIRS. IN JESUS' NAME. AMEN.**

ONE WAY

One thing that Christians have got to fall back on, though, is Jesus says that I am the way and the truth and the life.
—Johnny Cash

Jesus answered, "I am the way and the truth and the life. No one comes to the Father except through Me."
—John 14:6 niv

French philosopher Blaise Pascal theorized that we are all born with a God-shaped hole in our lives. It's a provocative and powerful image, and one that goes a long way toward explaining certain human behaviors. Think about it. Why are we so fascinated by the prospect of life after death? What compels us to look for meaning in this world? What inspires us to search for our purpose? Why do we need a reason for being here? Why are justice and fairness so important to us? Why is mercy so meaningful? Why do we long to be part of something bigger than ourselves?

The best explanation is a God-shaped hole in our lives. God created us to enjoy an intimate relationship with Him. So the things of God matter to us, whether we realize it or not. Until we're secure in that relationship, we'll continue to search for ways to connect with the Almighty.

Sin complicates our search more than we can possibly imagine. God, after all, is perfect. He can have nothing to do with sin. That's bad news for everyone who isn't perfect, because sin creates a chasm between us and God that we can't cross on our own. We're helpless to create the connection with God that we were made to enjoy.

Because God is perfectly just, the only payment He will accept for our sin is a perfect sacrifice. Our sin disqualifies us from making that sacrifice, so that leaves only Jesus. Jesus lived a sinless life. He is perfect in every way. Only His death could pay the price for our sin. Only His resurrection could make eternal life possible for us.

When we look to Jesus to save us from our sin, He reconnects us with God. He is the only One who can help us fill the God-shaped hole in our lives. Johnny Cash took comfort in that knowledge, and we can too. Our search for God ends when we find Jesus. So does our search for eternal life. And our search for meaning, purpose, and direction in this world. Jesus is the Source of all of it.

It's good news worth sharing. Some people spend their whole lives searching for something that will get them closer to God, something that will connect them to eternity. They explore ancient teachings and philosophies. They rely on rituals and ceremonies. They work hard to earn God's favor.

Yet the hole remains. So the challenge for those of us who have filled it is to help others do the same. We do that by helping them recognize Jesus' one-of-a-kind qualifications to connect us with God. By helping them see the beautiful simplicity of God's plan and the incredible sacrifice of Jesus that made it possible.

DEAR GOD, THANK YOU FOR SENDING JESUS TO BUILD THE ONLY BRIDGE POSSIBLE BETWEEN US AND YOU. THANK YOU FOR SACRIFICING YOUR SON SO THAT WE CAN HAVE THE HOPE OF ETERNAL LIFE. GIVE ME THE WISDOM AND OPPORTUNITY TO HELP OTHERS UNDERSTAND THAT JESUS ALONE IS THE WAY, THE TRUTH, AND THE LIFE. IN HIS NAME. AMEN.

PROMISES KEPT

*Through Him and a daily commitment to Him and His ways
makes me bear the pain a little better every day.*
—Johnny Cash

*For no matter how many promises God has made, they are "Yes" in Christ.
And so through Him the "Amen" is spoken by us to the glory of God.*
—II Corinthians 1:20 niv

Pain is a frequent companion in this world, as Johnny Cash well understood. Sometimes the difference between overcoming the pain and being overcome by it is knowing where to turn when it gets intense. Fortunately for us, God has stocked His Word with promises that we can cling to when everything else seems hopeless. Here are four of those promises that can help us bear our pain a little better every day.

One: "I will never leave you or abandon you" (Hebrews 13:5 csb). God doesn't promise to shield us from pain. He won't snap His fingers and make our lives pain-free. We live in a hurting world. If we don't know what it is to experience pain, we can't help other hurting people. And helping hurting people is one of our most important God-given assignments. But we will never have to face pain alone. God will not desert us in the midst of our struggles. Whatever we go through, God will be with us, always ready with His comfort, strength, and encouragement.

Two: "My grace is all you need. My power works best in weakness" (II Corinthians 12:9 nlt). The apostle Paul had prayed for God to remove "a thorn in my flesh" (II Corinthians 12:7 nlt)—something in his life that was making him miserable. This promise is part of God's refusal to give Paul what he wanted. God's point is that He will never give us more than *He* can handle.

Our strength and resilience ebb and flow; God's do not. And when we're at our weakest, God's strength is at its most apparent. So we're wise to turn to Him when things start to feel overwhelming and watch His strength flow through our weakness.

Three: "We know that all things work together for the good of those who love God" (Romans 8:28 csb). This is the essence of why we turn to God. He can take the bad things in our lives, as well as the worst elements of the world around us, and make something good from them. He can crack open a seemingly hopeless situation to reveal unmistakable rays of hope inside. He can make something extraordinary from lives that appear ruined. He can turn the page on what looks like an unhappy ending to reveal a promising sequel.

Four: "He will wipe every tear from their eyes" (Revelation 21:4 niv). Sadness is temporary for those who love God. Pain doesn't get the last word. Even in the darkest night of the soul, the light of hope shines. We can look forward, with hope and confidence, to living forever, with no sadness to endure and no pain to worry about.

If we embrace the promises of God long enough, an interesting thing happens. We begin to absorb their truth to the very core of our being. And we begin to radiate confidence, encouragement, comfort, and hope in the midst of our pain. As Johnny Cash points out, this daily commitment to God and His promises can gradually ease our pain or equip us to deal with it more effectively.

> **GOD, THANK YOU FOR THE PROMISES IN YOUR WORD. THANK YOU FOR GIVING ME SOMETHING TO HOLD ON TO WHEN MY PAIN GETS INTENSE. HELP ME KEEP YOUR PROMISES FRESH IN MY MIND. GIVE ME THE WISDOM TO APPLY THEM TO THE SITUATIONS I FACE. IN JESUS' NAME. AMEN.**

UNBURDENING

*If I can remember to turn my burdens over to Him
every day, the whole day goes a lot better.*
—Johnny Cash

*So humble yourselves under the mighty power of God, and
at the right time He will lift you up in honor. Give all your
worries and cares to God, for He cares about you.*
—1 Peter 5:6–7 nlt

Johnny Cash's candid admission raises an important question for all of us who wrestle with burdens that weigh us down. Why do we feel the need to carry them when we don't have to?

For some of us, it's a matter of pride. The myth of the superhero dies hard. We romanticize the notion of being the strong, silent type who perseveres, no matter what. The Wonder Woman who can do it all without breaking stride. We're told that self-reliance is part of becoming a mature adult. We celebrate athletes who play hurt and perform well under pressure. We work hard to emulate their example. We minimize our weaknesses and grow confident in our strengths. We revel in our ability to "bear up" when others crumble, even if it means ignoring glaring fault lines in our own mental health. We refuse to hand off our burdens because we can't imagine that anyone else can carry them as well as we do.

Some of us hold on to our burdens out of shame and embarrassment. We don't want others to know the things we struggle with. We become frozen by our fear of how people will react when they discover we're not as strong or as confident or as impervious to pain as we'd like them to believe. We resist asking for help because we don't want to be a burden. We figure everyone is struggling with their own challenges, so why should we add to their struggles by piling on our own burdens? Or we calculate that giving our burdens to others makes us beholden to them, and we get squeamish about being in someone's debt. Or we assume that it sets up a quid pro quo that allows others to share their burdens with us, and we're not sure we're up to the task.

Some of us hold on to our burdens out of ignorance or a lack of awareness. We simply don't realize how much emotional or spiritual weight we're lugging around. We don't recognize the toll it's taking on us. We write it off as the price of living in a broken world, assume everyone else is carrying similar burdens and do our best to get by. Or we underestimate God's willingness to take our burdens from us.

Every day our all-powerful heavenly Father sees us struggling with our burdens, worries, and cares, and He says, "Here, let Me help you with those." His help can come in any number of ways. He may give us peace of mind to come to grips with something that's troubling us. He may send someone into our lives with just the skills and strengths we need. He may change our circumstances. He may give us endurance when we need it most. All we have to do is ask Him and then give Him a chance to work.

> **HEAVENLY FATHER, THANK YOU FOR ALWAYS BEING READY TO CARRY MY BURDENS. THANK YOU FOR CARING ENOUGH ABOUT ME TO MAKE MY LOAD LIGHTER. REMIND ME OF YOUR STRENGTH EVERY DAY. BREAK THROUGH MY PRIDE, EMBARRASSMENT, AND IGNORANCE SO THAT I WILL LEARN TO TRUST YOU WITH MY BURDENS. IN JESUS' NAME. AMEN.**

THE HARDEST PERSON TO FORGIVE

I forgave myself. When God forgave me, I figured I'd better do it, too.
—JOHNNY CASH

He has removed our sins as far from us as the east is from the west.
—PSALM 103:12 NLT

It's tough to be our own worst critic. To obsess over mistakes that everyone else seems willing to overlook. To be haunted by past failures long after others have forgotten them. To see someone we don't respect every time we look in the mirror.

Yet that's what happens when guilt breaks free of its boundaries and runs rampant in our lives. We begin to fixate on the things we do wrong. We lose sight of God's grace. We find ourselves surrounded by reminders of our failures and bad choices.

The problem is compounded when our actions impact others. We face the anger, pain, and disappointment of the people we hurt. We must confront the broken trust and broken relationships that result. If we're not careful, our guilt and shame can overrun us.

Yet that's not what God wants. Not by a long shot.

In its proper place, guilt accomplishes a very important work. It serves as a warning to us that something is in the way of our relationship with the Lord. The Holy Spirit, who lives inside every Christian, speaks to us through our conscience, making us aware of things we've done.

He prompts us to ask God for forgiveness and then do the same with anyone who's been hurt by our actions. Once that work is done, once we sincerely seek forgiveness from God and others, guilt no longer has any place in our life.

God sets the parameters for us in Psalm 103. "As far as the east is from the west" is about as far as you can get. Yet that's how far God removes our sin from us—in His eyes. If we were to approach Him after being forgiven and ask, "God, do You remember when I—?" His response would be, "No, I don't." He chooses not to remember it.

So when we *choose* to remember it, when we insist on beating ourselves up for things in our past, when we refuse to let go of our guilt, we're actually holding ourselves to a higher standard than God uses. And we're missing out on one of the most glorious gifts that God offers.

When we learn to forgive ourselves, we start to see ourselves as God sees us. When we clear away the guilt and shame that no longer serve any purpose, we discover the potential hidden underneath. Self-loathing gets in the way of every good thing God has in store for us. Forgiveness frees us to be the people He intends us to be.

Forgiving ourselves makes it easier for us to forgive others. Grace and understanding, two of the most important tools for relationship-building, become more accessible to us. We're better able to empathize with other people's struggles to forgive themselves and more inclined to help them in their journey. So, in learning to forgive ourselves, we become better spouses, parents, friends, coworkers, and neighbors.

> HEAVENLY FATHER, THANK YOU FOR FORGIVING ME WHEN I STUMBLE AND FOR GIVING ME A FRESH START. GIVE ME THE WISDOM TO KNOW HOW TO SET THINGS RIGHT AND HOW TO MAKE NECESSARY CHANGES IN MY LIFE. LET YOUR SPIRIT WORK IN MY HEART SO THAT I CAN FORGIVE MYSELF AND SEE MYSELF AS YOU SEE ME. IN JESUS' NAME. AMEN.

LOCATING GOD

The Old Testament prophet Elijah reached his breaking point in the wilderness outside Beersheba. His faithful service to God had made him a marked man. A lonely, discouraged, frightened, marked man who could see no light at the end of his tunnel. The only prayer he could muster was for the Lord to take his life and end his misery.

God had a different idea. He directed Elijah to Mount Horeb, where the prophet found shelter in a cave. God then instructed Elijah to come out of the cave so that he could experience the rarest of privileges: a visit from God Himself.

As Elijah stood on the mountain, a powerful wind swirled all around him. The gusts were intense enough to shatter rocks. But God wasn't in the wind. An earthquake shook the very foundations of the mountain. But God wasn't in the earthquake. A roaring fire descended from heaven. But God wasn't in the fire.

After these three awe-inspiring phenomena came a still, small voice. Elijah recognized God's presence in it immediately. And if we learn to do the same, we can have the confidence that Johnny Cash talked about.

When our lives are knocked off-kilter by devastation, loss, fear, sickness, uncertainty, or countless other obstacles, our first instinct is to ask, "Where's God?" Our circumstances make us shortsighted. If we step back and look at the big picture, we discover that God is in everything good about our lives.

His fingerprints are everywhere. Sometimes, though, we allow them to go unnoticed. Or we give credit where credit isn't due. When seemingly insurmountable obstacles turn out to be minor inconveniences, we chalk it up to luck or an overreaction on our part. When someone intervenes on our behalf, we elevate them to near-hero status. When we persevere through pain and eventually find healing, we congratulate ourselves on our endurance.

Johnny Cash would urge us to look deeper into those circumstances—to dust for God's fingerprints.

God is in the unexpected development that cracks open a hopeless situation and allows rays of hope to shine through. God is in the friend who looks you in the eyes and says, "Tell me what's really going on with you." God is in that spark of resolve and strength that never gets extinguished—the confidence deep in your soul that, no matter how bad a situation may seem, you have what it takes to survive and thrive.

Every good and perfect thing in our lives comes courtesy of our heavenly Father. When we acknowledge that to Him, we strengthen our relationship. When we acknowledge it to ourselves, we will have a better understanding of our heavenly Ally, who is bringing about good from every bad situation.

FATHER, THANK YOU FOR THE GOOD THINGS IN MY LIFE. FORGIVE ME FOR THE TIMES I LOSE SIGHT OF YOU AND EVERY PERFECT GIFT YOU HAVE GIVEN ME. PLEASE GIVE ME THE SPIRITUAL VISION TO SEE YOUR HAND WORKING THINGS FOR GOOD IN MY LIFE, EVEN WHEN MY CIRCUMSTANCES SEEM BAD. IN JESUS' NAME. AMEN.

Just as I am, though tossed about
With many a conflict, many a doubt;
Fightings within, and fears without,
O Lamb of God, I come, I come!

—"Just as I Am" by Charlotte Elliott

WHAT'S HAPPENED TO YOU

If you're going to be a Christian, you're going to change. You're going to lose some old friends, not because you want to, but because you need to. You can't compromise some things. You have to draw the line daily—the line between what you were and what you're trying to be now—or you lose even their respect.

—Johnny Cash

Therefore, if anyone is in Christ, he is a new creation. The old has passed away; behold, the new has come.

—II Corinthians 5:17 ESV

Imagine going back to high school—or, better yet, grade school—in the same body you had back in the day, but with all the wisdom, knowledge, life experience, and maturity you have now. If you've seen the movie *Freaky Friday*, you already have a pretty good idea of the comic potential of the setup.

But what about the serious stuff? Imagine trying to pick up old friendships where you left off. Imagine trying to find common ground with people who hadn't changed at all—and who couldn't understand the changes in you. Imagine trying to enjoy things that used to seem fun but now hold little interest for you.

The only way to make the situation work would be to pretend that you hadn't changed. That you didn't have a whole new perspective on life. That you're still the same person you used to be.

Of course, even a great actor would have a hard time pulling that off. The differences between the old you and the new you would be too obvious to disguise.

The same holds true for someone who chooses to follow Christ. As the apostle Paul points out in II Corinthians 5, when we embrace Jesus as our

Savior and Lord, we are transformed and made completely new. Our old self passes away.

Though the transformation occurs inside us, the results are so profound and so undeniable that other people can't help but notice. And not everyone will be happy with the results. Some people will resent our new outlook and attitude. Some will accuse us as being hypocrites or thinking we're better than others. Some will make it clear that they liked the old version of us better. These are the reactions Johnny Cash warned about.

Pretending to be our old self isn't an option. The change inside us is too enormous to keep under wraps. Besides, no one really benefits when we try to be someone we're not.

The better option, as Johnny Cash points out, is to "draw the line daily" between who we are now and who we used to be. He urges us to lean into our new creation and embrace the transformation, for all to see.

Some old friends may cut ties with us, and that's heartbreaking. But if we remain true to our new nature, we may eventually win their grudging respect. Most people appreciate genuine integrity when they see it.

When we become a new creation, things can never be like they were before. But that's a good thing. Being a new creation opens a world of new opportunities. Our goal is to help others see that. We can be ambassadors for the new—even if it means ultimately sacrificing the old.

> **DEAR GOD, THANK YOU FOR TRANSFORMING MY LIFE. THANK YOU FOR GIVING ME A WHOLE NEW WAY OF LOOKING AT THE WORLD. GIVE ME THE STRENGTH AND COURAGE TO EMBRACE BEING A NEW PERSON, REGARDLESS OF THE FALLOUT. PLEASE HELP ME BE A LIGHT TO OTHERS SO THAT THEY CAN SEE YOUR TRUTH. IN JESUS' NAME. AMEN.**

THE POWER OF THE GOSPEL

In the Old Testament, God's people lived according to the Torah, also known as the law of Moses. The Torah was made up of 613 laws that guided the nation of Israel. God's people considered these laws sacred. So sacred, in fact, that well-meaning religious leaders created another set of rules, known as the Mishnah, to keep people from even coming close to breaking God's laws.

The Mishnah acted as a religious "fence" around the real law of Moses, a safety barrier to ensure that people didn't inadvertently wander into disobedience. For example, the law of Moses said, "Remember the Sabbath day, to keep it holy. . . . On it you shall not do any work" (Exodus 20:8, 10 ESV). The Mishnah identifies thirty-nine major categories—and hundreds of subcategories—of work that is forbidden on the Sabbath. Its rules are incredibly specific, down to how many steps a person can take and what a person is allowed to lift. All in an effort to keep the Sabbath holy.

Over time, the religious leaders of Israel placed more and more emphasis on the Mishnah until it became hard to separate the actual law of Moses from the human-made "safety barrier" rules. Worse yet, those same religious leaders began to judge people on their ability to obey these extra rules—that is, on their ability to follow impossibly complex instructions and so give the appearance of being holy.

A similar thing can happen with church doctrine, if we're not careful. The creeds and bylaws that govern churches were put in place by well-meaning people. Sincere differences in people's interpretations of the Bible led various congregations to spell out their doctrine so that others who interpreted Scripture in a similar way would have a place where they felt comfortable.

The problem is that, over time, doctrines tend to harden into purity tests or loyalty oaths. People with their own agendas try to weaponize doctrines to determine who's with them and who's against them.

Johnny Cash understood that doctrines are counterproductive when they become divisive. He found the gospel message to be not only more inclusive but also more direct. God loved *the world* so much that He gave His only Son to die in our place so that *anyone* who believes in Him will have eternal life. That was the message the Man in Black embraced and shared.

Certainly doctrines play a role in our walk with Christ. We need to be grounded in the core beliefs of our faith so that we can spot and call out false teachings. But the power of the gospel—the profound and simple message at the heart of our faith—can open doors and bring people together in ways that no other message can.

> **HEAVENLY FATHER, THANK YOU FOR THE SIMPLICITY OF THE GOSPEL MESSAGE. THANK YOU FOR OPENING THAT MESSAGE TO EVERYONE WHO WILL RECEIVE IT. PLEASE GIVE ME THE WISDOM TO COMMUNICATE YOUR MESSAGE IN A SIMPLE WAY AND THE DISCERNMENT TO RECOGNIZE THE IMPORTANCE OF CORE BELIEFS. IN JESUS' NAME. AMEN.**

LOUDER THAN WORDS

Telling others is part of our faith all right, but the way we live it speaks louder than we can say it. The gospel of Christ must always be an open door with a welcome sign for all.

—JOHNNY CASH

My friends, what good is it to say you have faith, when you don't do anything to show that you really do have faith? Can that kind of faith save you? If you know someone who doesn't have any clothes or food, you shouldn't just say, "I hope all goes well for you. I hope you will be warm and have plenty to eat." What good is it to say this, unless you do something to help? Faith that doesn't lead us to do good deeds is all alone and dead!

—JAMES 2:14–17 CEV

Most of us have developed a fairly sophisticated personal defense system. For better or worse, the more wisdom and experience we gain in our culture, the more sophisticated our defense systems become. We learn from an early age that not everyone can be trusted. Out of necessity, we create a radar to spot untruths, insincerity, and ulterior motives. We put up barriers to keep the "wrong" people from getting too close.

These defense systems create a problem for Christians who try to talk about our faith. People have heard the talk before. And they've also heard Scripture quoted to support various political positions. They've read un-Christlike social media posts by people who claim to follow Christ. They've paid attention to people who try to use God's Word for their own personal gain. They've watched as high-profile Christian leaders who preached moral responsibility fall from grace. The empty words of these and other believers have muddied the waters for anyone who would like to talk about what it means to be a Christian. They seem to confirm people's worst suspicions about our faith.

By the same token, these defense systems create an opportunity for people who prefer to demonstrate our faith in more tangible ways. Johnny Cash points out that if we really want to make our faith known, the best way to do it is through our daily actions. If we were merely talking about our faith, we would say, "Jesus made me a new person. He changed my life from the inside." Ho-hum. Maybe He did; maybe He didn't.

But when people see undeniable proof of a change in our lives, they're more likely to investigate the cause. Especially if those changes seem inviting and difference-making.

For instance, people notice when they see humility in situations where they expect to find pride and arrogance. When they see someone quietly helping someone in need. When they see someone take a stand for people who are being bullied or taken advantage of. When they see someone sacrificing their own needs and wants to provide for someone else. When they see someone extend loving-kindness and forgiveness—instead of vindictiveness and a judgmental spirit—toward someone who has wronged them.

A living faith—one that can't be expressed by mere words, one that pours out of us in every decision we make and every interaction we have—is the most powerful tool we have as believers. When we use it, people will notice.

FATHER, THANK YOU FOR SHOWING US YOUR LOVE THROUGH ACTIONS—FOR SENDING YOUR SON TO DIE IN OUR PLACE SO THAT WE CAN HAVE ETERNAL LIFE. GIVE ME THE COURAGE AND DISCIPLINE TO LIVE MY FAITH IN A WAY THAT'S BOTH NATURAL AND PUBLIC, SO THAT OTHERS CAN SEE WHAT THE GOSPEL OF CHRIST LOOKS LIKE. IN JESUS' NAME. AMEN.

THE JOURNEY 10

Every day is a brand-new mountain, and though you might feel
close to heaven today, tomorrow you can be down in the lowest
valley. It takes a lot of faith to walk daily with Jesus Christ.

—Johnny Cash

Where can I go from Your Spirit?
Or where can I flee from Your presence?
If I ascend into heaven, You are there;
If I make my bed in hell, behold, You are there.
If I take the wings of the morning,
And dwell in the uttermost parts of the sea,
Even there Your hand shall lead me,
And Your right hand shall hold me.

—Psalm 139:7–10 NKJV

Our daily walk with Jesus is unlike any other journey. There's no map, no apparent route, and no telling where it will end. And therein lies the adventure.

God invites us to embrace the journey itself, instead of getting caught up in trying to reach a destination. He encourages us to live in the moment every step of the way, instead of fretting about our progress. He doesn't want us to miss a thing.

Living in the moment means appreciating our Traveling Companion. God doesn't just wait on the mountaintops for us. He descends into every valley with us. He offers His hand for support when the road gets rocky. He shines a light at the end of every tunnel. We have the choice of whether to acknowledge

His presence or reach for His hand or look for His light along the way. But if we don't, we create a lonely journey for ourselves.

On the other hand, if we do choose to acknowledge Him, we'll find that He's not just our Traveling Companion; He's also our Travel Guide. He has planned our journey. We can't see where we're going, but He can. And He's chosen the ideal route for us.

As Johnny Cash points out, faith is the key to a fulfilling itinerary. Faith is saying to God, "I don't know where we're going, but I'm excited for the journey because I know You're taking me where I need to go." Faith allows us to live in the moment, to appreciate the journey itself.

Part of living in the moment is realizing that every stop along the way is temporary. The highest highs of mountaintop experiences can energize us, in proper doses. Any longer, they can exhaust us. Or leave us unprepared for the descent. The pits of the valley may feel interminable, but they're not. If we follow God's lead and double down on our faith in Him, we will find many paths out of our valleys. Some may take longer than others. Some may require a great deal of effort. But they're accessible to us.

Part of living in the moment is realizing that no matter where we are on our journey, other people are there too. God leads us into other people's orbits for a reason. We sharpen each other. Improve each other. Encourage each other. Challenge each other. Support each other. We lighten one another's loads. We make one another's journeys more manageable.

No matter where you are on your journey right now, embrace it. Think of the experiences and challenges God has brought you through and the people He's brought into your path. And then prepare yourself for the adventure ahead!

> HEAVENLY FATHER, THANK YOU FOR THE JOURNEY YOU'VE SET OUT FOR ME AND FOR THE PLEASURE OF YOUR COMPANIONSHIP EVERY STEP OF THE WAY. HELP ME FEEL YOUR PRESENCE, NOT JUST ON THE MOUNTAINTOPS AND IN THE VALLEYS, BUT IN THE IN-BETWEEN PARTS OF THE JOURNEY. STRENGTHEN MY FAITH SO THAT I CAN LIVE IN THE MOMENT THROUGHOUT MY TREK. IN JESUS' NAME. AMEN.

WRONG THINKING

*To repent and reform all the way to righteousness requires a
man to first recognize and admit he has been all wrong.*

—Johnny Cash

*But if we confess our sins to God, He can always be
trusted to forgive us and take our sins away.*

—I John 1:9 CEV

How many ways are there to say "I was wrong"?

There's the no-harm, no-foul approach: "My bad."

There's the it-could-have-been-a-lot-worse approach: "At least I didn't
_____."

There's the we're-all-in-this-together approach: "I'm not the only one
at fault."

There's the tempered-expectations approach: "I never claimed to be perfect."

There's the admit-no-legal-responsibility approach: "Mistakes were made."

And there's the nonspecific, noncommittal approach: "Oops."

Three simple, one-syllable words. Yet anyone who's ever tried to say them
with any sincerity knows how difficult it can be. Few other trios of words carry
the weight that "I was wrong" carries. Few others carry the implications that "I
was wrong" carries. Few others make us as vulnerable as "I was wrong" does.

When we admit to other people that we've done or said something wrong,
we risk our pride. We risk our dignity. We risk losing moral high ground.
We risk our reputation. We risk our self-image. In some cases, we risk public
shaming or humiliation.

Yet the payoff is worth the risk. We are most useful to God when we are
stripped of our pride and dignity. Our moral high ground is an anthill com-

pared to God's moral high ground. Our reputation and self-image mean something only when they factor into our relationship with God. And being publicly shamed and humiliated for doing the right thing puts us in some pretty good company, starting with Jesus and working through countless heroes of the Christian faith.

God urges us to be transparent about our failures and shortcomings so that other people can see His grace and forgiveness at work in our lives. Admitting that we're wrong may make us vulnerable, but it also makes us relatable. People can empathize with mistake makers and wrongdoers. If we have the courage to embrace the role, and—this is key—if we sincerely work to make amends for our wrongdoing and take the necessary steps to avoid repeating our mistakes, we can point the way forward for other hurting people. We can introduce God's forgiveness to those who desperately need to experience it.

Being able to say, "I was wrong," also keeps our relationship with God healthy and vibrant. God wants us to feel the weight of our wrongdoing. Not because He wants us to suffer, but because He wants us to fully appreciate His forgiveness and grace.

Forgiveness is a healing ointment that works best on a raw wound. The more deeply we feel our wrongdoing, the more deeply we feel God's forgiveness. The more deeply we regret our broken relationship with God, the more deeply we appreciate its healing.

When we deny doing anything wrong, when we make excuses for what we've done, when we argue that our wrongdoing pales in comparison to others', or when we try to minimize the impact of what we've done, we allow our wrongdoing to scab over. The result is a hardened shell that blocks God's forgiveness. When we own up to our wrongdoing with honesty and brokenness, we tear off the scab and allow God's forgiveness to do its cleansing work.

FATHER, YOUR FORGIVENESS IS TOO AMAZING FOR ME TO FULLY UNDERSTAND. BUT I PRAISE YOU FOR IT. PLEASE WORK THROUGH YOUR HOLY SPIRIT TO MAKE ME AWARE OF TIMES WHEN I FAIL YOU. GIVE ME THE CHANCE TO SAY, "I WAS WRONG," AND HELP OTHERS DISCOVER YOUR FORGIVENESS AND GRACE. IN JESUS' NAME. AMEN.

STILLING THE VOICES

*When the raging voices quieted and the evil presences left me,
there would move in gently about me a warm, sweet presence,
and a still, small voice would breathe forth inside my being: "I am
your God. I am still here. I am still waiting. I still love you."*
—JOHNNY CASH

*For I am convinced that neither death nor life, neither angels nor
demons, neither the present nor the future, nor any powers, neither
height nor depth, nor anything else in all creation, will be able to
separate us from the love of God that is in Christ Jesus our Lord.*
—ROMANS 8:38–39 NIV

*You're not good enough.
You don't measure up.
You're not worthy of love.
The road ahead is too difficult for you.*

When messages like these come from other people, they can throw us off
our game or make us question ourselves. But when messages like these come
from inside us, they have the potential to dominate our interior monologue.
In extreme cases, they can paralyze us emotionally—or make us do things we
later regret. Johnny Cash's description of them as "raging . . . evil presences"
hints at their power.

Yet Johnny Cash knew from personal experience that these malevolent,
lying, troublemaking voices can be stilled. He identifies four truths about God
that are more powerful than any other voice in our lives. The first truth is "I
am your God." God has sovereign control over everything. No voice is pow-

erful enough to overrule His verdict on us. And the sovereign Creator of the universe sees us as valuable, important, and so worthy of love that He gave His only Son to save us.

The second truth is "I am still here." God isn't going anywhere. The voices give us reason to fear being abandoned. After all, if we're truly as unlovable, unworthy, or unmemorable as they want us to believe we are, who would want to stay with us? Yet God flips the narrative by saying, "I do." He sees us at our worst, when the voices are raging, and says, "I still want to walk with you every step of the way." We may choose to walk away from Him, but He will never walk away from us.

The third truth is "I am still waiting." God is patient with us. Not only does He see us at our worst, but He also sees the best within us. He sees our potential. He knows exactly what we're capable of. And He waits patiently for us to discover it. If there's one thing most of the heroes of the Bible have in common, it's that they didn't discover the hero within right away. In fact, many of them looked to be hopeless cases at the outset. Yet God remained patient with them and eventually guided them into situations where they could realize their potential.

The fourth truth is "I still love you." As the apostle Paul makes clear in Romans 8, nothing can separate us from God's love. We can build our foundation on it. It's that solid. When certain areas of our lives seem unstable, we can find our footing on God's love. He loves us and sees the best in us. We should do the same.

> **HEAVENLY FATHER, THANK YOU FOR QUIETING THE VOICES THAT CAUSE ME TO DOUBT MYSELF OR QUESTION MY WORTH. WHEN DOUBT AND UNCERTAINTY START TO CREEP INTO MY LIFE, REMIND ME THAT NOTHING CAN SEPARATE ME FROM YOUR LOVE. GIVE ME THE WISDOM AND OPPORTUNITY TO SHARE THE GOOD NEWS OF YOUR LOVE WITH OTHERS WHO NEED TO HEAR IT. IN JESUS' NAME. AMEN.**

THE GOD WHO UNDERSTANDS

God is love and God is forgiving. He'll forgive you seventy times seven and seventy times that. He is long-suffering, patient, compassionate, and He understands even before you try to explain your weaknesses and shortcomings to Him.

—Johnny Cash

For You, Lord, are good, and ready to forgive, and abundant in mercy to all those who call upon You.

—Psalm 86:5 nkjv

Few things take us out of our comfort zones like the need to apologize. First, there's the realization that we've done something serious enough to warrant an apology. That stomach-churning recognition that our wrong was too big to let slide or to laugh off. That awareness that we crossed a line we shouldn't even have approached.

Second, there's the feeling of regret that invades our consciences, that fervent wish to take back our words or actions. With those pangs of regret comes the realization that the only way forward—the only way to clear our consciences—is to acknowledge what we've done and ask for forgiveness.

Third, there's that giant swallow of pride that goes before an apology. A genuine apology requires us to take complete ownership of our wrong actions. It doesn't allow us to save face by making excuses, shifting blame, or gaslighting others. We have to acknowledge our failure.

Fourth, there's the vulnerability of placing ourselves at someone else's mercy. There's no way of knowing how someone will respond to our apology. We have no guarantees that someone will give us forgiveness when we ask for it.

As Johnny Cash points out, the one exception to this rule involves God

Himself. Every day brings opportunities big and small to ignore God and pursue our own desires. To do things that require us to seek His forgiveness.

Yet our heavenly Father has already removed the drama and suspense from the process. His answer to us is never in doubt. So the extraordinary situation we face is that the One we have wronged is also the One who, more than anyone else, wants to see us succeed. God is our biggest Cheerleader. He's the One standing in our corner telling us, "You can do this," after everyone else has left. He's the One who urges us not to allow ourselves to be defined by our failures.

Though He is hurt by our wrongdoing, His love surpasses that hurt. So when we come to Him with sincere regrets about what we've done and a sincere desire to turn away from it, He stands ready to forgive. To wipe our slates clean.

Jesus called His disciples to forgive others not "up to seven times, but up to seventy times seven" (Matthew 18:22 NKJV). God, however, forgives us completely the first time we ask.

He understands the temptations we face. He understands our weaknesses and shortcomings. His patience is never exhausted. He sees the incremental growth and maturity taking place within us. He sees us slowly learning from our past mistakes. And He works to foster our growth. So every time we approach Him, sincere in our desire for His forgiveness, He will forgive.

> **FATHER, THANK YOU FOR ALWAYS BEING MY BIGGEST CHEERLEADER. YOU UNDERSTAND ME BETTER THAN ANYONE ELSE DOES. NO MATTER HOW MANY TIMES I STUMBLE, YOU PICK ME UP, DUST ME OFF, AND SET ME IN THE RIGHT DIRECTION AGAIN. GIVE ME THE WISDOM AND HUMILITY TO TURN TO YOU FOR FORGIVENESS EVERY TIME I STUMBLE SO THAT I CAN ALWAYS STAY CLOSE TO YOU. IN JESUS' NAME. AMEN.**

THE PROWLING ENEMY

When you stand with Him, you must renew the stand daily; you must daily be on guard. The hounds of hell are not going to stop snapping at your heels. The devil and his demons aren't going to give up on you as long as they can find a vulnerable spot once in a while.

—Johnny Cash

Be alert and of sober mind. Your enemy the devil prowls around like a roaring lion looking for someone to devour.

—I Peter 5:8 niv

The devil takes on many forms in popular culture. The horror movie villain who sheds his benign human appearance in the film's climax to reveal his actual form—a fire-spewing CGI demon-dragon. The smiling, fire-engine red, two-horned proprietor of hell who welcomes newcomers with malevolence-tinged courtesy before revealing their (usually ironic) eternal fate. The shady dealmaker who's always ready to offer wealth, fame, and talent in exchange for people's souls.

The reality is a little more complex. Satan, as portrayed in the Bible, doesn't announce his presence with a fiery display of demonic power. He isn't found in hell. He doesn't obtain souls through contractual trickery.

Instead, he displays the instincts of an animal predator. The serpent in the garden of Eden. The roaring lion in I Peter 5. He doesn't overpower. He doesn't try to match strength for strength. Instead, he prowls. He observes. He waits. He plots.

He looks for vulnerabilities in his prey, weaknesses he can exploit. In the garden of Eden, he probed Adam and Eve's understanding of God's command ("Did God really say. . . ?"; Genesis 3:1). When he saw a vulnerability, he pounced with his tempting offer.

Johnny Cash recognized his strategy. So did the apostle Peter, who knew all too well what it was like to have his vulnerabilities exploited. Both men offer similar advice for dealing with such an insidious enemy. "Be on guard." "Be alert and of sober mind."

Notice that both are preemptive strategies. Once the devil locks on to one of our vulnerable areas, through temptation or some other means, we're at a disadvantage. That doesn't mean we can't still resist him. It just makes the battle that much more difficult.

The wiser strategy is to anticipate enemy attacks so that we're prepared to counter them. We do that by identifying our vulnerable areas—the temptations we're most susceptible to, the people who bring out the worst in us, the situations that cause us to lower our guards. The better acquainted we are with our own weak areas, the better we can anticipate our enemy's likely moves against us.

Once we know where we're vulnerable, we can ask God to help us shore up those areas. We can strengthen our defenses through prayer and the wisdom of God's Word. We can learn to avoid situations that put us at risk. We can draw on God's power to thwart the devil's battle plan. We can be confident in the Lord's ability to see us through any situation.

We have no reason to fear Satan's power. First Peter 5:8 says, "Be alert," not, "Be afraid." But we should anticipate and prepare for it. With God's help, we can blunt the impact of Satan's attacks.

> HEAVENLY FATHER, BECAUSE OF YOU I DON'T HAVE TO FEAR MY ENEMY. THANK YOU FOR BEING MY MOST IMPORTANT ALLY IN MY BATTLE AGAINST THE DEVIL. PLEASE GIVE ME THE SELF-AWARENESS TO RECOGNIZE MY VULNERABLE AREAS AND THE STRENGTH TO SHORE THEM UP. HELP ME PREPARE FOR SATAN'S ATTACKS BEFORE THEY COME. IN JESUS' NAME. AMEN.

The high and lofty one
who lives in eternity,
the Holy One, says this:
"I live in the high and holy
place with those whose
spirits are contrite and humble. I restore the crushed
spirit of the
humble and revive the
courage of those with
repentant hearts."

—Isaiah 57:15 NLT

THE PROBLEM WITH PRIDE

*My man-pride and arrogance vanished the minute
I humbled myself enough to call on Him.*
—Johnny Cash

Pride leads to disgrace, but with humility comes wisdom.
—Proverbs 11:2 nlt

Pride is the trickiest of wrongs because it usually feels right. It doesn't set off alarms inside us. A conscience in good working order will alert us when we lie, cheat, steal, gossip, or hurt others. When we get caught in the act doing those things, we feel remorse, shame, and embarrassment. Pride, on the other hand, has a cloaking device that allows it to slip past our conscience's radar.

Sometimes pride looks and feels like moral rightness. We make daily choices to honor the Lord. We obey the commands in His Word, as we understand them. We try to follow Jesus' example. Understandably, we see ourselves as doing the right thing and living the right way. And we're given an opportunity to elevate ourselves in our own eyes, while at the same time rethinking our attitude toward others. After all, if we're *right*, doesn't that make those who challenge or disagree with us *wrong*?

Sometimes pride looks and feels like a passion for God's work. We invest ourselves in the lives of others and involve ourselves in worthy ministries. And, once again, we're given an opportunity to elevate ourselves—this time, in the eyes of others. It seems natural to want to publicize our ministry efforts. Harmless humblebrags here and there that seem to give glory to God, but also manage to shine a light on our own goodness. Social media posts that draw attention to our servant's heart.

A little self-promotion may seem harmless enough, but it actually creates obstacles in our relationship with God. Our pride robs Him of glory that is rightfully His. After all, we're able to serve Him only because He equips us and gives us the opportunity to do so. We're able to make godly choices only because He destroyed the power of sin over us. He alone deserves the praise.

When we allow pride to get a foothold in our lives, we become God's competitors, challenging Him for His glory and honor. And that's not a role to embrace.

Pride also limits our usefulness to God. The Bible describes the relationship between God and His human creation as that of Potter and clay. God shapes us, like a potter shapes clay, so that we can be of maximum use to Him. Every part of our design is intended for a specific purpose. What's more, we're a continuous work in progress. God shapes us day by day, and sometimes even moment by moment, to fit our changing circumstances.

The more pliable we are, the more effectively God can mold us. And the key to our pliability is humility—the humble spirit that comes from recognizing ourselves for what we are: lumps of clay being molded into something extraordinary by the Master Potter. We can give thanks for what God does in and through us, but we can't take credit for it. We can't take pride in it.

Johnny Cash recognized not only the danger of pride but also the limitless potential of humility. A humble spirit opens up a world of possibilities to us.

FATHER, THANK YOU FOR YOUR MASTERFUL CRAFTSMANSHIP IN MY LIFE. I AM WHO I AM BECAUSE YOU CREATED ME THIS WAY. PLEASE GIVE ME THE SPIRITUAL VISION TO RECOGNIZE PRIDE BEFORE IT TAKES ROOT IN MY LIFE. SHOW ME WHAT A HUMBLE SPIRIT LOOKS LIKE SO THAT I CAN STAY PLIABLE IN YOUR HANDS. IN JESUS' NAME. AMEN.

A DANGEROUS FOE

There are two powerful forces in the world—the forces of right and wrong, or the forces of good and bad. I choose to call it the force of God and the force of the devil. The number-one power in this world is God. The number-two power is Satan, and though he manages to fight for second in my life . . . God is the victor in my life. I'd be nothing without Him. I want to get in a good lick for Number One.

—JOHNNY CASH

So humble yourselves before God. Resist the devil, and he will flee from you.

—JAMES 4:7 NLT

The most dangerous enemy is the one who has nothing to lose. That's Satan. He should have known his plan was doomed to fail when he led one-third of the angels in heaven in a rebellion against God. He should have known that his limited strength was hopelessly overmatched by God's limitless power. But he was blinded by pride and a lust for power. His defeat was swift, but not quite final. So he bided his time, waiting for another opportunity.

He saw a glimmer of hope when God created the human race. Exploiting the gift of free will that God gives every person, Satan coaxed Adam and Eve into defying the Creator's command not to eat from one specific tree in the garden of Eden. The enemy of God no doubt celebrated his role in the fall of humankind.

With every subsequent sin, Satan gained power and influence. In the New Testament, he is referred to as "the god of this world" (II Corinthians 4:4 NLT), "the prince of the power of the air" (Ephesians 2:2 NKJV), and "the ruler of this world" (John 12:31 NKJV). But then came the Son of God.

Jesus' birth marked the beginning of the end of Satan's reign, whether Satan realized it or not. Jesus came to earth as fully God and fully human. He experienced the same kinds of trials and temptations that everyone else experiences. Yet Jesus never once succumbed to His trials. He never once gave in to temptation.

Just before Jesus started His public ministry, Satan appeared to Him in the wilderness. Three times the devil tempted Jesus to veer from the course that God had set for Him. Three times Jesus rebuffed Satan by quoting God's Word. It would be the first of several more defeats for the devil.

Jesus lived a sinless life. In doing so, He broke the power of sin—and Satan—forever. After He gave His life to save the world, Jesus rose from the dead. In doing so, He broke the power of death—Satan's ally—forever.

Jesus' sinless life, sacrificial death, and triumphant resurrection ended the war between God and Satan. Satan was defeated. However, he remains free to do battle until God's final judgment. And that's what makes him such a dangerous force. He has nothing to lose. He just wants to do as much damage as possible while he can.

Ultimately, however, God's power in our lives keeps the enemy in check. He can mislead us, but he can't overcome us. As Johnny Cash points out, God has won the victory in our lives. The only thing Satan can do is disrupt the celebration.

> **FATHER, THANK YOU FOR BEING NUMBER ONE IN MY LIFE. THANK YOU FOR DEFEATING SATAN THROUGH THE SACRIFICE OF YOUR SON. HELP ME MINIMIZE SATAN'S POWER IN MY LIFE BY STAYING CLOSE TO YOU AND YOUR WORD. IN JESUS' NAME. AMEN.**

SOMETHING TO BELIEVE IN

There is no fence to sit on between heaven and hell. There is a deep, wide gulf, a chasm, and in that chasm is no place for any man. And I must pity those who say they don't believe in God. Even the devil believes in God.

—Johnny Cash

You believe that there is one God. Good! Even the demons believe that—and shudder.

—James 2:19 NIV

For someone who has a thriving, personal relationship with God, the thought of someone not even being able to acknowledge His existence can be baffling. How can someone else look at the same universe, the same natural world, the same daily miracles of life that we look at and not see evidence of the Almighty everywhere?

Yet the reality is that most of us likely know several people who identify as atheists or agnostics. And that raises a question for those of us who identify as believers. What should be our response to our acquaintances who don't believe in God or who aren't interested in the question of His existence?

Johnny Cash uses the word "pity," and that's a great place to start. People who don't believe in God deserve our compassion and understanding, and not our opposition. Atheists and agnostics aren't our enemies. They're the people God wants us to love. (And even if they were our enemies, our assignment wouldn't change. Jesus tells us to love our enemies.)

One way we can show love is by serving as a sounding board for them. Instead of arguing, debating, or trying to change their minds, we can listen. We can invite them to talk about how they came to their (non)belief. We can listen with compassion and empathy as they share the circumstances that led to their decision not to believe in God.

Some people may talk about growing up in an atheistic or agnostic household. Others may talk about a personal tragedy that made them reconsider the existence of a loving God—or any God. Still others may talk about having their views about God changed by a particular book, teacher, or mentor.

Whatever the case, if we withhold judgment and resist the urge to try to reframe their story or change their perspective, we earn the right to share our own story. We can talk about our personal experiences with God, the times when we experienced His presence in unmistakable ways. We can be open about our own doubts and struggles. But we can also talk about what God means in our daily life.

A spirit of humility will go a long way toward keeping the lines of communication open. And an open line of communication is essential, because "proving" the existence of God is not our ultimate goal. As Johnny Cash points out, even the devil believes in God. And as the New Testament writer James points out, even demons believe in God.

Believing in God's existence is a necessary first step. But it's only a first step. Our ultimate aim is to help people to build a personal relationship with God. And Jesus is the One who makes such a relationship possible.

> HEAVENLY FATHER, THANK YOU FOR MAKING IT SO EASY NOT JUST TO BELIEVE IN YOU BUT ALSO TO HAVE A PERSONAL RELATIONSHIP WITH YOU. PLEASE WORK IN THE LIVES OF MY FRIENDS AND ACQUAINTANCES WHO STRUGGLE TO BELIEVE. MAKE YOURSELF KNOWN TO THEM. HELP ME MAKE YOU KNOWN TO THEM THROUGH MY OWN RELATIONSHIP WITH YOU. IN JESUS' NAME. AMEN.

WALKING A FINE LINE

*Once a Christian puts himself above the world, or in his
fervor becomes "holier than thou" or too good to associate
with people of questionable character, then he has alienated
the very people who need what he has to share.*
—JOHNNY CASH

*Since God chose you to be the holy people He loves, you must clothe yourselves
with tenderhearted mercy, kindness, humility, gentleness, and patience.
Make allowance for each other's faults, and forgive anyone who offends you.
Remember, the Lord forgave you, so you must forgive others. Above all,
clothe yourselves with love, which binds us all together in perfect harmony.*
—COLOSSIANS 3:12–14 NLT

God's people walk a fine line. On the one hand, we're instructed to live our lives in a way that reflects God's work in our lives. Often this requires us to approach life from a perspective that other people don't share. It sets us on a path apart from others, one that often runs against the crowd. Our Christian faith sets us apart. The New Testament calls us aliens, strangers in a strange land, not of this world.

On the other hand, we have to stay relatable. Other people need to see themselves in us. They need to know that what's happened in our lives can happen in theirs. If we get too otherworldly, we risk . . . well, *alienating* the very people we're called to serve.

In his letter to the Colossian believers, the apostle Paul identifies five qualities that keep us grounded and help us build genuine connections with the people we serve. The first is tenderhearted mercy. In order to show tenderhearted mercy to the people God puts in our lives, we have to look past the things that cause friction or disconnects in our interactions with them. Differing personalities, viewpoints, backgrounds, and circumstances tend to cloud our vision of other people. In order to see them more clearly, we have to consider the unspoken struggles they're facing—the fears, anxieties, and insecurities they wrestle with.

When our hearts are tender, we're more apt to show the second quality: kindness. The great thing about kindness is that it can be customized to fit any personality and any situation. For some, kindness might look like picking up a neighbor's trash after her garbage can is knocked over. For others, it might look like stopping to talk to the guy holding a sign on a street corner. And for others, it might look like buying a holiday-inspired latte for the impatient person in line behind you at the coffee shop.

The third quality is humility. This gets to the heart of what Johnny Cash was talking about. Everything that makes a Christian special comes from Jesus, not us. It's important that we communicate that truth. As the old saying goes, "A Christian is just one beggar telling another beggar where to find food."

The fourth quality is gentleness, showing genuine care and respect to others in the way we act and speak. Jesus set the standard for gentleness in His interactions with people. A gentle spirit earns people's trust.

The fifth quality is patience. Patience sends the signal that we're invested in others for the long haul, that we have no timetable or agenda. Patience allows others to feel comfortable with us and helps establish a lasting bond.

> **FATHER, THANK YOU FOR ENTRUSTING ME TO SHOW OTHERS YOUR LOVE. LET YOUR HOLY SPIRIT WORK IN MY HEART SO THAT MERCY, KINDNESS, HUMILITY, GENTLENESS, AND PATIENCE BECOME SECOND NATURE TO ME. BLESS MY EFFORTS TO REACH OUT TO OTHERS. IN JESUS' NAME. AMEN.**

FAIL-SAFE

*I am not so sure of myself that I think I'm too strong to fall.
I know that I can't always, and won't always, resist every
temptation. I know the dangers of walking through dark valleys,
and when I do so, the Shepherd is never too far away.*

—Johnny Cash

*My flesh and my heart may fail, but God is the
strength of my heart and my portion forever.*

—Psalm 73:26 niv

Failure is a lonely business—especially in our culture, where success is the only thing that matters. When we succeed, everyone wants a piece of the glory. People are eager to jump on our bandwagon. They want to say they played a role in our success—or, at least, they were somehow connected to it.

But failure isolates us, especially if our failure becomes public knowledge. People try to keep a strategic distance from failure—close enough to get the details, but far enough away to keep from being tainted by it. Failure invites ridicule and judgment.

So it's sobering to admit, as Johnny Cash did, that no matter how strong and confident we may seem, we're never more than one bad decision or one moment of weakness away from failure. Like him, we know the dangers of walking through dark valleys. We're all too aware of the wrong paths that beckon us away from the light. We know which temptations don't always get resisted.

So the specter of failure looms large, as do the feelings of disappointment, discouragement, embarrassment, and loneliness that follow. And if we're not careful, we can lose sight of the truth that Johnny Cash celebrates: that we're never actually alone. The reality is, not everyone recoils from failure. In fact, there is One who steps closer to us when others step away. Jesus assures us that failure doesn't decrease our value in His eyes. In fact, if our failure is handled properly, it actually makes us more valuable to Him. It gives us perspective and hard-earned wisdom that can be extremely useful in reaching out to others.

Like a shepherd with his sheep, Jesus nudges us back on to the right path after our failure. He leads us to a place of rest and nourishment. He cares for us.

When the healing process is complete, He sends us out to act as shepherds for others who are feeling lost and alone after their own failures. Johnny Cash never shied away from talking about his failures—or about the Shepherd who walked with him through the dark valleys. In being so open about his struggles, he helped knock down the barriers of judgment, loneliness, and isolation that come with failure.

We can do the same. We can be the people who demonstrate God's love to others who are struggling in the wake of failure. We can be the Lord's "first responders," the ones who move toward the crisis while other people are moving away from it.

We can establish a connection with hurting people by being transparent about our own experiences with failure. We can share how God strengthened us and helped us recover. We can stand by these people when others won't. And we can point them to the One who will walk with them through their dark valley.

> **HEAVENLY FATHER, THANK YOU FOR NEVER GIVING UP ON ME. THANK YOU FOR STANDING BY ME WHEN I FAIL. FORGIVE ME FOR WHEN I FAIL YOU. HELP ME LEARN AND GROW FROM MY MISTAKES. USE ME AS AN INSTRUMENT OF HEALING, SUPPORT, AND ENCOURAGEMENT FOR OTHERS WHO HAVE FAILED. IN JESUS' NAME. AMEN.**

BENEATH THE GLITTER

Satan is the great imitator, the great counterfeiter, and he can make anything look beautiful and right. In seeing through his imitations, in acknowledging my mistakes and shortcomings, in denouncing, rebuking and rejecting what I sincerely believe is wrong for me—in daily contact with the Counselor—I get a better definition of what really is beautiful and right.
—Johnny Cash

There is a way that seems right to a man, but its end is the way to death.
—Proverbs 14:12 esv

All that glitters is not gold" seems like a sufficient warning: not everything that appears valuable really is. The problem is, we have an enemy who glitter-bombs almost everything in our paths. He can make anything seem valuable, worthwhile, and compelling. The key word, of course, is *seem*. Look again at Johnny Cash's description of Satan: "the great counterfeiter."

King Solomon, one the wisest people who ever lived, expresses the same idea in Proverbs 14:12 csb: "There is a way that *seems* right to a person" (emphasis added).

Satan is all about surface grandeur. He entices us to pursue things that seem golden—or right—at first glance. And if we don't pause to scratch the surface—if we don't consider carefully what we're pursuing—we can get sidetracked from God's plan for us.

Perhaps the most dangerous aspect of Satan's counterfeiting skills is his ability to make an empty life seem fulfilling. He convinces us that wealth will bring us happiness. He encourages us to measure our worth according to our worldly success and power. He tricks us into believing that fame and celebrity are worth any sacrifice we need to make to achieve them. It's only later, after we've wasted our time and energy, and after we've sacrificed things we wish we hadn't, that we discover Satan's ruse.

As Johnny Cash points out, the best way to avoid being left sadder but wiser by Satan's counterfeit schemes is to stay "in daily contact with the Counselor." The closer we stay to God, the less likely we are to wander down a dead-end path. God works through His Word and His Holy Spirit, who lives inside every believer, to help us see past Satan's glitter and lies.

God has filled the pages of Scripture with nuggets of wisdom and guidance far more valuable than anything Satan tempts us with. In the Old and New Testaments, He shows us people who obeyed and followed Him—people who made His priorities their priorities—and who reaped the benefits of their decisions. He also shows us people who rejected His guidance, pursued their own agendas, and ultimately paid the price for it. Even better, He gives us a specific blueprint to follow in the life of His Son. Everything we need to know about choosing substance over flash we can find in Jesus' words and actions.

Meanwhile, God's Holy Spirit mans the controls of our hearts and consciences, guiding us down the paths He would have us go and warning us when we veer off course. He helps us spot counterfeits. He draws our attention to the empty places inside us—the absence of genuine fulfillment—that result from pursuing hollow accomplishments. He creates in us a yearning for something real, something substantial, something that truly matters. And, as Johnny Cash said, He helps us see "what really is beautiful and right."

> **HEAVENLY FATHER, THANK YOU FOR LAYING BEFORE ME A PATH THAT WILL LEAD TO GENUINE FULFILLMENT. THANK YOU FOR GIVING ME TREASURE WHOSE VALUE FAR SURPASSES ANY COUNTERFEIT SATAN HAS TO OFFER. GIVE ME THE WISDOM TO SORT THE GOLD FROM THE GLITTER. HELP ME RECOGNIZE MY ENEMY'S LIES. IN JESUS' NAME. AMEN.**

30

GRABBING HOLD

The Carpenter and I have established a line of communication—a kind of bond, and the bond has stood many tests and trials. He and I both know that many more trials will come, but He makes me know that because I am truly committed, that I profess Him and let Him know I need Him, He won't let me slip too low or slide too far before He grabs hold again.

—Johnny Cash

Then Peter got down out of the boat, walked on the water and came toward Jesus. But when he saw the wind, he was afraid and, beginning to sink, cried out, "Lord, save me!" Immediately Jesus reached out His hand and caught him.

—Matthew 14:29–31 niv

The kind of bond Johnny Cash talks about can be seen in Peter's relationship with Jesus. Their bond endured more than a few tests and trials. And in one dramatic encounter, Peter discovered that Jesus would not let him slip too far.

The incident took place at sea. Peter and the other disciples were making a night crossing. In the middle of their journey, a huge wind kicked up. Waves pounded the vessel, threatening to capsize it. To add to the terror, the disciples saw someone walking toward them on the surface of the water.

Their fears eased when they recognized the figure as Jesus. Suddenly emboldened, Peter asked to join Jesus. Jesus invited him onto the water, so Peter jumped overboard and walked toward the Lord.

Just for a moment, Peter stopped to consider the situation. He felt the wind and saw the waves. And he started to sink. But Jesus didn't let him go under. He grabbed Peter's hand and refocused his attention—away from the things that frightened him and back on Himself.

This extraordinary encounter offers some important takeaways that can strengthen our own bond with Jesus. First, Jesus rewards humble boldness. Peter didn't jump out of the boat to get attention. Or because he thought it would be fun to walk on water. He did it because he wanted to be closer to Jesus.

Peter left the relative safety of his immediate circumstances to do something that others wouldn't. Something that seemed risky to the people around him, but not to Peter, because His focus was on Jesus. And Jesus rewarded him with an absolutely unforgettable experience. A similar reward awaits everyone who steps out in faith.

The second takeaway is that Jesus didn't calm the winds to make Peter's walk easier. Instead, He helped Peter walk in the midst of the tumult. Likewise, Jesus will not make our journey wave-free. Trials strengthen us, toughen us, and deepen our relationship with the Lord. They also prepare us to help others who struggle. Jesus will not deprive us of these growth opportunities.

Jesus also let Peter feel the sensation of sinking. Peter took his eyes off the goal—off Jesus—and focused on the dangers and obstacles that surrounded him. And he momentarily paid the price for his distraction. Yet with a single cry, "Lord, save me!" Peter restored the connection. Jesus reached out to help him regain his footing. And He will do the same for anyone who cries out to Him in the midst of a trial.

HEAVENLY FATHER, THANK YOU FOR MAKING THE BOND POSSIBLE WITH YOUR SON. THANK YOU FOR THE EXTRAORDINARY OPPORTUNITIES YOU GIVE ME TO "STEP OUT ONTO THE WATER" WITH HIM. GIVE ME THE COURAGE TO LEAVE MY SAFETY ZONE AND THE DISCIPLINE TO KEEP MY FOCUS ON JESUS AS I DO. IN HIS NAME. AMEN.

WHERE YOUR TREASURE IS

I must keep priorities in order.
I must weed out the commitments I make that are not
a part of what He really wants me to do.
—Johnny Cash

Where your treasure is, there your heart will be also.
—Luke 12:34 csb

Priorities are funny things. Often other people can recognize them before we can.

The Bible doesn't tell us specifically how to order our priorities, but it does give us direction. In Luke 12:34 csb, Jesus says, "Where your treasure is, there your heart will be also." This cuts through the self-deception that a lot of us practice.

When we talk about priorities, we often share our idealized version: God first, family second, job third, ministry fourth, working out fifth, recreation sixth—or some variation thereof. We want to believe that our strong feelings about God and family reflect themselves in the way we order our time.

But that's not always the case. The priorities we announce aren't always the priorities we live. Jesus points out that where our heart is—that is, where we devote our actual time, energy, and thought—reveals what we truly treasure. We can't hide behind platitudes or good intentions. We can't make a distinction between quality time and quantity time.

The only accurate way to determine priorities is to turn a critical eye to our daily routines. All we need is a way to record what we do from the time we get up to the time we go to bed—and the courage to do so honestly, without trying to affect the outcome. We can use an app, a spreadsheet, or a journal and pen. What's important is that we report our time objectively.

Beyond that, we can talk to friends whose opinions we value—accountability partners who aren't afraid to speak truth to us. We can ask them to share their reading of our priorities, based on the time they spend with us.

Most importantly, we can spend time in God's presence, asking for His input on our priorities. In quiet solitude, we can pray and then listen to Him with an open heart as He reveals truths about us that we may not be aware of ourselves. We can let Him convict us of priorities that don't reflect His own.

An honest assessment of our priorities can be startling. And embarrassing. And motivating.

Priorities can be changed. Johnny Cash talks about weeding out the commitments that were not a part of what he really wanted to do. We can do the same. It comes down to making conscious decisions, instead of allowing inertia or pressure from others to monopolize our time.

One other thing to consider is Jesus' words in Matthew 22:36–40. When someone asked Him what the greatest commandment is—that is, the thing that should be our highest priority—Jesus said we must love God and love our neighbor.

Of course, it's hard to calculate the amount of time we spend loving God or showing love to the people around us. So perhaps a better approach is to make sure that in every priority, we do what God would have us do and show generous love to the people around us.

> **HEAVENLY FATHER, THANK YOU FOR MAKING ME A PRIORITY. THANK YOU FOR HELPING ME UNDERSTAND THE IMPORTANCE OF ESTABLISHING THE RIGHT PRIORITIES IN MY LIFE. GIVE ME THE COURAGE AND STRENGTH TO SAY NO TO CERTAIN THINGS IN MY LIFE SO THAT I CAN GIVE A HIGHER PRIORITY TO THE THINGS THAT REALLY MATTER. IN JESUS' NAME. AMEN.**

Amazing grace! how sweet the sound,
That saved a wretch like me!
I once was lost, but now am found,
Was blind, but now I see.

—"Amazing Grace" by John Newton

WALK THIS WAY

*I have no greater joy in my salvation than to
hear that my children walk in truth.*
—Johnny Cash, quoting III John 4

*Train children to live the right way, and when
they are old, they will not stray from it.*
—Proverbs 22:6 NCV

For most parents, the realization sets in the first time they hold their new-born. *This child—this beautiful miracle of creation—is utterly dependent on me for protection, guidance, and direction. The way this young person ultimately sees the world, approaches life, and makes key decisions will be shaped in large part by me.*

That awareness can be overwhelming. Responsibilities don't come much bigger than parenthood (or anytime when you are influencing a child's life). But neither do opportunities. And that's what God has given us: an extraordinary opportunity to introduce our children to Him and His will for their lives.

We get to influence the way they think of Scripture. We get to show them how to communicate with the Creator of the universe. We get to open their eyes to the gifts of God that surround us every day.

And in return, as Johnny Cash points out, we get to share in the joy of their salvation and in the work that God does in and through them.

Being an influence in a way that pleases God and keeps our children on the path that He has laid out begins with a simple realization. We need to recognize that we are being watched. We may not always be aware of it. Our kids may not even be aware of it. But they are watching. They watch the way we process anger, sadness, frustration, and fear. They watch the way we treat the people we love and the people we are not particularly fond of. They pay attention to the things we watch, read, and listen to.

They are looking to us for direction, whether they care to admit it or not. The world can be a confusing and scary place. Having the right guides can make it much less so. Let's seize the opportunity our kids give us.

We do that by living our faith in big ways and small. By talking about the choices we face. By intentionally choosing God's way. By being vocal about the positive consequences we experience for choosing God's way.

We do that by staying disciplined. By letting our habits, priorities, and interactions reflect our walk with Christ. By letting the kids in our lives see that God's Word is the highest authority.

If our kids see in us a vibrant, powerful relationship with God that makes a real difference in our lives and in the lives of the people in our orbit, they will be more likely to follow our lead and build their own relationships with God. Maintaining that kind of consistency in our walk with Christ creates a real challenge for us. But it's one of the most rewarding challenges we'll ever rise to.

By sharing God's love with the children in our lives, we leave a gift that will outlast us. When they're old, their relationship with God will still be guiding them—and perhaps influencing the next generation. Or two.

HEAVENLY FATHER, THANK YOU FOR THE WISDOM OF YOUR WORD. THANK YOU FOR SETTING BEFORE US A PATH THAT WILL LEAD TO ULTIMATE HAPPINESS AND FULFILLMENT. GIVE ME THE CONFIDENCE TO EMBRACE THE CHALLENGE AND OPPORTUNITY THAT YOU HAVE GIVEN ME. IN JESUS' NAME. AMEN.

CARETAKERS

You get in trouble when you go against nature—
and God is the Father of mother nature.
—JOHNNY CASH

The LORD God put the man in the Garden of Eden
to take care of it and to look after it.
—GENESIS 2:15 CEV

Guardians of the planet. Caretakers of the earth. Protectors of the natural realm. Whatever name we choose for ourselves, the fact remains that we have a God-given responsibility to tend to the earth and everything in it.

The mandate is nearly as old as creation itself. God created a paradise for the human race to enjoy. He stocked it with a breathtaking array of flora and fauna. Fruit trees bursting with luscious sustenance. Flowers and plants of indescribable beauty. Animals that would one day be predator and prey roamed the grounds in peaceful cohabitation. Nature in perfect harmony.

God created a place so beautiful, so inviting, that He Himself spent time there, walking in the cool of the evening with Adam.

This perfect environment was a gift from our Creator—and a responsibility from Him, as well. Tending to it, keeping it beautiful, harvesting its fruits, and prioritizing its care became our occupation. It was work He created us to do. It was a way for us to find fulfillment.

Adam and Eve's decision to disobey God and eat from the one tree in the garden that was off-limits to them brought down a curse on them and the natural world. Paradise came to an end. But our responsibility to care for our environment did not.

We are still the caretakers of the earth. Sure, the job became a lot more challenging in the wake of Adam and Eve's sin. But we still have an opportunity to fulfill one of our very first God-given assignments.

The first step involves an internal reckoning. We acknowledge and embrace our responsibility. Through prayer, Bible study, and interaction with other believers, we formulate some practical notions of what being a caretaker looks like on a daily basis. We learn to see the natural world around us as being under our care. We nurture a heart for its well-being.

God didn't create the earth for our pleasure and exploitation. All created things belong to Him. He created them to fulfill His purposes. Our job is to sustain, protect, and enhance His creation for His glory. The fact that we also benefit from that work is evidence of God's grace.

The second step is to start locally in our stewardship. This involves taking the time to educate ourselves on the wisest course of action for managing our local natural resources, as well as the healthiest ways to care for our yards, our neighborhoods, and our communities. We can join with other conscientious stewards to make real changes in our communities.

From there, we can expand our efforts and support organizations looking to make a difference on a bigger scale. We can be the caretakers our Creator calls us to be.

HEAVENLY FATHER, THANK YOU FOR CREATING SUCH AN INCREDIBLE HOME FOR US ON THIS PLANET. THANK YOU FOR THE BEAUTY OF YOUR CREATION AND THE WAY IT SHOWS YOUR PERFECT PLAN FOR US. THANK YOU FOR ENTRUSTING US WITH ITS CARE. SPEAK TO MY CONSCIENCE SO THAT I CAN RECOGNIZE MY RESPONSIBILITY AS A CARETAKER. GIVE ME THE WISDOM TO KNOW HOW TO PROTECT AND INTERACT WITH YOUR CREATION IN A WAY THAT PLEASES YOU. IN JESUS' NAME. AMEN.

SEND ME

*Then I heard the Lord asking, "Whom should I send as
a messenger to this people? Who will go for us?"
I said, "Here I am. Send me."*
—Isaiah 6:8 nlt

God appeared to Moses from a burning bush in the wilderness. He had startling news. The time had come for the Israelites to be freed from slavery in Egypt, and God had chosen Moses to lead them out.

Moses didn't need to be told how big this opportunity was. The journey out of Egypt would take God's people through the wilderness to a land of their own. The Promised Land. The land flowing with milk and honey. The place where all Israelites longed to be.

The person who led this journey would carve a place for himself in Israel's history. His name would be revered for generations. He would serve as a spokesman for the Almighty.

God gave Moses a glimpse of the divine empowerment he could expect as leader of the exodus. He performed two miracles involving Moses' staff and hand.

Moses took a moment to consider the undeniable miracles he'd just witnessed, the appearance of God Himself in a bush, the wretched conditions and desperate plight of the Hebrew slaves, and the unprecedented opportunity that had been laid out before him. Then he said to God, "Pardon Your servant, Lord. Please send someone else" (Exodus 4:13 niv).

Moses couldn't envision himself in that role. He was slow of speech, totally wrong for the job. He couldn't see what God saw in him. It didn't occur to him that the events in his life had been preparing him for this moment.

To be fair to Moses, that kind of humility and self-doubt are part of God's grand plan. If we're too confident in our own ability, we're less likely to stay close to Him and more likely to claim credit for ourselves. God wants humble submission. He wants to make sure that credit for His work goes to Him and Him alone. So Moses passed that test.

But what he didn't understand is that there's no second-guessing when the Lord calls us to do something. Unlike in the corporate world, there's no mystery as to whether the right person has been chosen for the job. God knows exactly how we're wired because He did the wiring. He knows exactly what we're capable of. And He doesn't call us to fail.

Moses' situation was unusual in that he got a glimpse of the big picture of God's plan. God rarely offers such glimpses—and for good reason. If He laid out His entire plan for us, our heads would explode.

So He gives us just enough information, just enough strength, and just enough courage to get us from point A to point B. And when He's ready for us to move to point C, He gives us what we need to get there. Eventually, if we stay close to Him and follow His lead, we will find ourselves in a position to accomplish something extraordinary, sometimes whether we realize it or not.

So when God's call comes, our best response is to echo the words of the prophet Isaiah: "Here I am. Send me."

FATHER, THANK YOU FOR THE CONFIDENCE YOU PLACE IN ME WHEN YOU CALL ME TO SERVE YOU. THANK YOU FOR SEEING QUALITIES IN ME THAT I CAN'T SEE MYSELF. WORK IN MY SPIRIT. MAKE ME AWARE OF YOUR PRESENCE. LEAD ME ON AN ADVENTURE THAT WILL ACCOMPLISH YOUR WORK. IN JESUS' NAME. AMEN.

BY THE GRACE OF GOD

*We must place ourselves entirely in God's hands and
rely upon His grace to live the true life.*
—Johnny Cash

*Let us then approach God's throne of grace with confidence, so that we
may receive mercy and find grace to help us in our time of need.*
—Hebrews 4:16 niv

Grace is a pocketknife word; it is multifunctional. It communicates a sense of elegance or rhythmic style ("She has the grace of a ballerina"). It can refer to a polite courteousness ("He had the grace to apologize before he left"). It can even serve as a synonym for prayer ("Don't forget to say grace before you eat").

The sense in which Johnny Cash and the writer of Hebrews use the word, however, is much more profound. Grace, in this context, refers to the undeserved gifts that God showers on us. Sometimes His grace is unmistakable and life-altering. Often, however, His grace is so constant and so pervasive that it becomes part of the fabric of our lives. And if we're not careful, we may start to take it for granted.

In his quote, Johnny Cash speaks of being mindful—not just of grace, but also of our responsibility to place ourselves in God's hands and of living a life that embraces His truth.

When we place ourselves entirely in God's hands, we stop relying on our own strength and wisdom. We acknowledge the superiority of God's plan for us. We spend more time listening in prayer than we do making requests. We stay attuned to the Holy Spirit's work in our conscience. Hardest of all, we give God those little pieces of ourselves that we desperately want to hold back—the habit we can't quite kick, the grudge we refuse to let go of, the ambition that gets us into trouble. We surrender those things to our heavenly Father.

Relying on God's grace requires us to have a sense of how God works. His grace can take on many forms when it's filtered through people's individual circumstances. When the Israelites suffered from dehydration and thirst on their journey through the wilderness, God's grace looked like water flowing from a rock in the middle of the desert. When Shadrach, Meshach, and Abednego faced their crucible, God didn't make His grace known until they were in the midst of the fire. When Paul was struggling with what he called a "thorn" in his "flesh," God showed His grace not by removing the thorn, but by helping Paul see how that thorn made him a more effective minister for Christ. The more we study God's Word and talk to God's people about evidence of His grace in their lives, the better equipped we'll be to rely on His grace in our own lives.

The challenge of living a true life is that it may not be the life we envision for ourselves. It may fall short of our expectations for wealth, fame, and prestige. That's when we must approach the throne of God with confidence, to ask our heavenly Father to help us embrace the life He has mapped out for us. After all, the reward of a true life is the kind of fulfillment that no other life can offer.

> **FATHER, YOUR GRACE IS TRULY AMAZING TO ME. THANK YOU FOR THE UNDESERVED GIFTS YOU SHOWER ON ME. GIVE ME THE COURAGE TO PLACE MYSELF ENTIRELY IN YOUR HANDS, THE AWARENESS TO RECOGNIZE YOUR GRACE IN MY LIFE, AND THE DISCERNMENT TO LIVE IN A WAY THAT IS TRUE. IN JESUS' NAME. AMEN.**

ROOTED IN LOVE

Our life is to be rooted in love. We are ever indebted to
always love our neighbor, and we must never stop.
—Johnny Cash

"So now I am giving you a new commandment: Love each other.
Just as I have loved you, you should love each other. Your love for
one another will prove to the world that you are My disciples."
—John 13:34–35 nlt

Surface-y love is easy, isn't it? Most of us can hold a smile, maintain eye contact, and nod empathetically long enough to make a good impression. We know how to give the appearance of loving concern in short bursts of social interaction, whether we genuinely feel that love or not.

But that's not what Jesus calls us to. Nothing about His love is surface-y or contrived. He's not concerned about making an impression on other people; He's concerned about making a difference in their lives. Look at the bar He sets for the way we're to love others: "just as I have loved you."

Think about the impact Jesus' love has had on your life. His love gives you hope. His love assures you that you're not alone. His love encourages you to step out in faith, maximize your God-given gifts, and grow in your relationship with Him. That's the impact we should be striving for in the way we show love to others.

Johnny Cash exposes the difference between surface-y love and impactful love with a single word: *rooted*. The kind of love Jesus calls us to comes from deep within us. Its roots run to the core of our being.

Before such roots can grow, however, we must plant spiritual seeds. We do that by studying Jesus' example, the way He interacted not just with His disciples but also with random people He encountered on His journeys. We do that by exploring our spiritual gifts, understanding better how God has equipped and wired us. We do that through prayer, constant communication with our loving heavenly Father. We do that by watching the example of others, mature believers who have mastered the art of Christlike love.

When our seeds bear fruit, they create a win-win-win scenario for everyone involved. The kind of love Jesus calls us to makes a difference in the lives of the people who experience it firsthand. They get a sense of what it's like to have someone care deeply for them, with no ulterior motives. They see themselves as being worthy of love.

The kind of love Jesus calls us to makes a difference in our lives as well. Following Jesus' example in showing love to others brings us closer to Him. The intimacy it creates extends into other areas of our lives as well. A loving spirit will help change the way we approach our own struggles. It will result in a healthier self-image. It will change the way others see and interact with us.

The kind of love Jesus calls us to also makes a difference in the lives of others who witness it. Even though they're not experiencing it firsthand, they're seeing Jesus' love at work. They're seeing what it looks like to be His disciple. They're seeing something that can change their lives. The fact that we have an opportunity to give them such a glimpse is another of God's loving gifts to us.

HEAVENLY FATHER, THANK YOU FOR THE LOVE YOU SHOW ME. THANK YOU FOR ENTRUSTING ME WITH YOUR LOVE, SO THAT I CAN SHARE IT WITH OTHERS. HELP ME RECOGNIZE THE OPPORTUNITIES I HAVE TO DO JUST THAT. NOURISH THE ROOTS OF MY SOUL SO THAT I CONTINUE TO PRODUCE THE FRUIT OF LOVE AND DISCIPLESHIP. IN JESUS' NAME. AMEN.

EXPECTING THE UNEXPECTED

Live for Jesus as if He's coming today.
—Johnny Cash

*"So you also must be ready, because the Son of Man will
come at an hour when you do not expect Him."*
—Matthew 24:44 niv

There's a popular T-shirt that reads, "Jesus is coming. Look busy." While the message is intended to be irreverent, it's not far from the truth that Johnny Cash expresses. All we have to do is substitute the word *Get* for *Look*.

Jesus' coming is one of the most mysterious events in all of Scripture. Christians differ in their interpretations of the passages that describe it. Two things virtually all of us can agree on are that Jesus is coming back and that His followers have a God-given responsibility to fulfill in the meantime.

Jesus said to His disciples, "Do not let your hearts be troubled. You believe in God; believe also in Me. My Father's house has many rooms; if that were not so, would I have told you that I am going there to prepare a place for you? And if I go and prepare a place for you, I will come back and take you to be with Me that you also may be where I am" (John 14:1–3 niv).

I will come back. Those words are true because Jesus spoke them. He is God; He cannot lie. His promises can be trusted.

People still doubt, of course. People have been raising doubts about Jesus' return since the moment He left. Two thousand years later, the chorus grows even louder: If Jesus is really coming back, why hasn't He done it already?

Here's how the apostle Peter answers: "The Lord is not slow in keeping His promise, as some understand slowness. Instead He is patient with you, not wanting anyone to perish, but everyone to come to repentance" (II Peter 3:9 niv).

God's delay of Jesus' return isn't due to forgetfulness, busyness, disinterest, or a desire to heighten anticipation. His motivation is love. He wants to give as many people as possible time to repent and come to Jesus.

With this in mind, how should we spend our time during this delay? How can we, as Johnny Cash says, live for Jesus as if He's coming today?

Here are three places to start. First, don't get wrapped up in the "when." Matthew 24:36 makes it abundantly clear that no one except God the Father knows when Jesus will come back. Of course, that hasn't stopped countless would-be prophets from offering their predictions. In extreme cases, these "prophets" have led people dangerously and destructively astray. Yet even in the most harmless cases, they've wasted people's time. We have more important things to consider.

Second, stay close to Jesus. We do that through prayer, Bible study, and following His example in our daily thoughts, actions, choices, and priorities. The closer our relationship is with Him, the sweeter our reunion will be when we're reunited.

Third, considering the reason for God's delay, share the good news of Jesus with as many people as possible. Look for opportunities to talk about your faith with the people in your orbit. Make an eternal difference in people's lives so that they, too, can look forward to Christ's return.

> **HEAVENLY FATHER, I PRAISE YOU FOR THE TRUTHFULNESS OF YOUR WORD. I TRUST YOUR PROMISE THAT JESUS WILL COME AGAIN. THANK YOU FOR YOUR LOVING DELAY. GIVE ME THE WISDOM AND DISCERNMENT TO KNOW HOW TO MAKE THE MOST OF YOUR DELAY—HOW TO ACCOMPLISH YOUR WILL IN THE MEANTIME. IN JESUS' NAME. AMEN.**

TAKING IT PERSONALLY

I'm thankful for a pair of shoes that feel really good on my feet; I like my shoes. I'm thankful for the birds; I feel like they're singing just for me when I get up in the morning, saying, "Good morning, John. You made it, John." I'm thankful for the sea breeze that feels so good right now, and the scent of jasmine when the sun starts going down. I'm thankful.

—JOHNNY CASH

I will give thanks to the LORD because of His righteousness; I will sing the praises of the name of the LORD Most High.

—PSALM 7:17 NIV

Johnny Cash's lyrical way of describing his thankful spirit can lull us into believing that it's something casual and unstudied—something that comes naturally. In reality, developing a thankful spirit is a lifelong effort that involves observation, acknowledgment of God's work in this world, and no small amount of discipline.

The first step in developing this spirit is observing. At any given moment, we have dozens of things vying for our attention. Some are important; most are distractions. In order to nurture a thankful spirit, we have to purposefully redirect our focus. We do that by putting away our devices, spending time in nature, reconnecting with old friends, and countless other ways. And then we observe. We look at the world around us with curiosity.

The second step is to take our observation a little further and notice the work of God in the things we see. We can start with nature. We can find beauty in everything from sunsets to sea breezes to the scent of jasmine. We can also find evidence of God's grand design in the way He provides for creatures great and small.

Beyond nature, we can consider God's work in our lives. The people He's brought into our orbit. The skills He's blessed us with. The struggles He's walked us through. Not every blessing is immediately recognizable as a blessing. Some can only be seen after the fact. What looks like an insurmountable obstacle can turn out to be an instrument of growth for us. That's why it's important to continuously consider what we have to be thankful for.

The third step is to express our gratitude. We do that in prayer through praise and thanksgiving. The more personal we are in our expressions, the more meaningful they are—to God and to us. For an idea of what a personal expression of gratitude to God looks like, reread Johnny Cash's quote. We can also express our thankfulness in our conversations with others. We can talk about the things we've observed and considered. We may even inspire others to focus on their own spirit of thankfulness.

The final step is to record our observations. Journaling is one of the most valuable spiritual disciplines available to us. If we nurture a journaling habit by writing even a little every day about the things we have to be thankful for, we'll have a record of our spiritual growth that may be valuable to us someday. When we face difficulties or doubts, we can look back at our journals to remind us of the various ways God has blessed us.

> **HEAVENLY FATHER, THANK YOU FOR SURROUNDING ME WITH SO MANY REMINDERS OF YOUR LOVE. WHEREVER I LOOK, YOUR BLESSINGS ARE THERE. I ASK YOU TO HELP ME SEE MORE OF THEM. OPEN MY EYES TO THE MANY WAYS IN WHICH YOU CARE AND PROVIDE FOR ME. DEEPEN MY APPRECIATION FOR THE BEAUTY AND WONDER OF CREATION. CREATE IN ME A SPIRIT THAT PRAISES YOU CONTINUOUSLY. IN JESUS' NAME. AMEN.**

THE MEASURE OF TRUE STRENGTH

*The strong are those who welcome the weak in a spirit
of toleration and sympathy, not judging.*
—JOHNNY CASH

*My friends, we beg you to warn anyone who isn't living
right. Encourage anyone who feels left out, help all
who are weak, and be patient with everyone.*
—I THESSALONIANS 5:14 CEV

What does it mean to be strong? Some people work their entire lives to build physical strength. They push their bodies to the limit to maximize its potential. Others strive to build their intellectual strength. They approach life as a constant quest to gain and apply knowledge. Still others pride themselves on their emotional strength. Perhaps they've survived difficulty in their past and have emerged stronger for it.

Not all strength is obvious. But all strength is potent. Strength—whether physical, intellectual, or spiritual—sets us apart. It's a resource that not everyone possesses. If you see yourself as strong in one or more of these areas, you're faced with a choice. Do you use your strength for yourself or for others?

The temptation to use it for your own gain is understandable. You're the one who put in the work. You're the one who persevered through tough times. Why shouldn't you be the one to benefit from the results? What's wrong with indulging in a little ego boosting? Why shouldn't strong people bask in their strength?

Johnny Cash hints at the answer in his quote. If we use our strength for nothing else than to enhance our own reputation or to satisfy our own needs, we're missing out on an untold number of God-given opportunities.

Think about it. Who is the strongest person ever—physically, intellectually, *and* emotionally? Hint: He exercised power over sickness and death. He engaged the wisest, best educated, and most respected scholars of His time in debate and emerged victorious every time. He suffered more intensely than anyone who ever lived, yet still had the emotional strength to forgive His enemies in the midst of His pain.

Perhaps the most awe-inspiring display of Jesus' strength, however, took place on a boat at night on the open sea. A furious squall blew up and threatened to swamp the vessel that Jesus and His disciples were in. Jesus stood up and said, "Quiet! Be still!" Immediately the wind stopped blowing and the sea turned calm (see Mark 4:35–41).

Yet that doesn't tell the whole story. Jesus didn't display His power for His own benefit. He had nothing to gain by calming the storm. He was asleep on the boat; the storm didn't bother Him. But His disciples were terrified. And their weakness caused them to seek out Jesus' strength.

Using His power to benefit the powerless was one of Jesus' highest priorities on earth. Look at the list of people He singles out for care in Matthew 25:31–46: those who are hungry and thirsty, strangers, those who have no provisions, those who are physically incapacitated, and those who are imprisoned. His focus was on helping the weak, and not on flexing His muscles.

Each of us has strength to give. Jesus calls us to follow His example in using our strength to better the lives of those who are weak. If we heed His call, we will discover what true strength can accomplish.

HEAVENLY FATHER, I PRAISE YOU FOR YOUR STRENGTH. YOUR POWER IS GREATER THAN THE UNIVERSE. YET YOU USE IT TO HELP THOSE IN NEED. GIVE ME THE WISDOM TO FOLLOW YOUR EXAMPLE, TO USE WHATEVER STRENGTH I HAVE TO HELP THOSE WHO ARE WEAKER. HELP ME MAKE A DIFFERENCE IN THEIR LIVES FOR YOUR GLORY. IN JESUS' NAME. AMEN.

THE ART OF DECREASING

The great principle in all matters is, "Not 'I,' but 'Christ.'"
—Johnny Cash

"He must increase, but I must decrease."
—John 3:30 esv

John the Baptist was a pretty big deal in first-century Israel. He fulfilled Old Testament prophecy as the forerunner of Christ. He built a large following with his baptism ministry in the wilderness. His unusual style of dress and eating habits increased his notoriety. And when Jesus began His public ministry, He sought out John to baptize Him.

The temptation for John to embrace and capitalize on his fame must have been enormous. Certainly his followers were eager for him to do just that. But John understood his place. More importantly, he understood Jesus' place.

When his followers complained that Jesus' ministry was drawing people away from his own, John showed his remarkable grasp of God's plan. He also showed remarkable understanding of how to find ultimate fulfillment and joy in life.

John's reply to his disciples concerning Jesus—"He must increase, but I must decrease"—shares spiritual DNA with the guiding principle of Johnny Cash's life—"Not I, but Christ." Both acknowledge that we were never meant to be at the top of our own priority list. That's not where God intends us to be. If we try to occupy that position, our relationship with Christ will suffer. We will miss out on the fulfillment and joy that He has in store for us.

So we must learn to rethink the way we approach daily life. Our desire to pursue our own agenda must decrease; our desire to pursue the Lord's will must increase. Our willingness to give in to temptation must decrease; our God-honoring self-control must increase. Our concerns about what other people will think of us must decrease; our efforts to deepen our relationship with the Lord must increase.

If we look to John the Baptist as a role model, we should also be aware that the process of decreasing himself and increasing Jesus was a struggle even for him at times. John faced a tough road. His fearlessness in his ministry got him in trouble. Herod Antipas, the ruler of Galilee, imprisoned the prophet for condemning Herod's marriage to his brother's former wife. John languished in jail for over a year. During that time, he wrestled with doubt. He also learned that most people in the region had rejected Jesus as the Messiah.

He sent disciples to ask Jesus one very specific, very pointed question: Are You who You claim to be? He was ready to give Jesus first place in his life—after he got some reassurance from the Lord.

Jesus didn't object to the question. He didn't excoriate John for his doubt. Instead, He offered the reassurance that John was looking for. He said what He needed to say to comfort John and to prove Himself worthy of being given first priority in John's life.

He does the same for us. Reducing our role in our own lives is a tall order. Jesus understands that. He spent thirty-three years as a human, dwelling on earth with us. He experienced what we experience. So He's ready with reassurances, as well as with rewards, when we put Him first.

HEAVENLY FATHER, THANK YOU FOR GIVING US AN EXAMPLE IN YOUR WORD OF HOW TO PUT JESUS FIRST IN OUR LIVES. GIVE ME THE WISDOM TO RECOGNIZE WHEN THERE IS TOO MUCH "I" IN MY PRIORITIES. HELP ME LEARN TO DECREASE IN A WAY THAT HONORS YOU SO THAT CHRIST CAN INCREASE IN MY LIFE. IN JESUS' NAME. AMEN.

GETTING CREATIVE 41

My way of communicating with God as a boy (and often even
now) was through the lyrics of a song. . . . So I didn't have the
problem some people do who say, "I don't know how to pray." I
used the songs to communicate with God. . . . To me, songs were
the telephone to heaven, and I tied up the line quite a bit.

—JOHNNY CASH

Shout with joy to the LORD, all the earth!
Worship the LORD with gladness.
Come before Him, singing with joy.
Acknowledge that the LORD is God!
He made us, and we are His.
We are His people, the sheep of His pasture.
Enter His gates with thanksgiving;
go into His courts with praise.
Give thanks to Him and praise His name.
For the LORD is good.
His unfailing love continues forever,
and His faithfulness continues to each generation.

—PSALM 100:1–5 NLT

In four sentences, Johnny Cash offers a revealing glimpse into his formative years, his relationship with God, and his personality. It's not hard for us to imagine him drawing closer to the Lord through music. Truth be told, most of us probably would have loved to have been a fly on the wall during Johnny's private conversations with the Lord.

Johnny Cash also reveals something of God's grace to us. He confirms what the writer of Psalm 100 understood: that God is pleased by our genuine efforts to praise and draw near to Him. As long as those efforts come from an attitude of worship and reverence, it doesn't matter to Him what form they take. Johnny Cash used the musical voice God blessed him with to deepen his relationship with his heavenly Father. We're free to do the same, even if our musical voice sounds nothing like Johnny Cash's. God cares about the gladness and joy in our spirits, not the technical prowess of our voices.

Of course, music is just one way to incorporate our creative gifts into our relationship with our Creator. We might also use our writing skills to work poems, psalms, or journal entries into our worship. We might use our artistic talent, expressing our praise through painting or drawing. Any creative endeavor that honors God or calls attention to His perfections or His work in this world is open to us. The possibilities are limited only by our imaginations.

There's one more aspect of Johnny Cash's quote that bears mentioning. As a boy, he sang for an audience of one. The more he sang, however, the more his talent grew. He expanded his audience. His skill at interpreting the music and lyrics of others eventually led him to write his own lyrics. Johnny Cash used his God-given talents to worship God. God, in turn, used Johnny Cash's God-given talent to inspire others. Millions of people have found comfort, solace, and connection with God through Johnny Cash's songs.

Likewise, as we hone our own creative skills through worship, we may have the opportunity to inspire or enhance other people's worship. When we plant the seed of creativity in our personal worship time, there's no way of telling how it will blossom. But it will bear fruit. And it will make a difference.

HEAVENLY FATHER, I PRAISE YOU FOR THE PRIVILEGE OF ENTERING YOUR PRESENCE. THANK YOU FOR CREATING IN ME A UNIQUE WAY TO EXPERIENCE THE WORLD AND YOUR BLESSINGS. THANK YOU FOR THE FREEDOM TO PERSONALIZE MY TIME WITH YOU. BLESS MY EFFORTS TO PRIORITIZE MY PRAYER TIME SO THAT I MAY CONTINUE TO GROW IN YOU. IN JESUS' NAME. AMEN.

Then sings my soul,
my Savior God, to Thee:
How great Thou art!
How great Thou art!

—"How Great Thou Art"
by Stuart K. Hine

DOING WHAT OTHERS WON'T

*Christianity should spread the joy of righteous love,
compassion, and consideration for others.*
—Johnny Cash

*Since God chose you to be the holy people He loves, you must clothe
yourselves with tenderhearted mercy, kindness, humility, gentleness, and
patience. Make allowance for each other's faults, and forgive anyone who
offends you. Remember, the Lord forgave you, so you must forgive others.*
—Colossians 3:12–13 NLT

From the outset of his career, Johnny Cash cut a path that often ran contrary to prevailing attitudes. He wasn't afraid to swim against the current. Or to set a higher standard for himself and others. Or to espouse values that seemed old-fashioned or passé.

In this single sentence, he called himself, and all believers, to a lifestyle marked by three qualities that are in short supply in our culture. He recognized that these three qualities will set Christians apart from the crowd and make us vulnerable to the slings and arrows of those who don't share our priorities. But he also understood the life-changing difference these qualities can make in other people's lives.

Righteous love is unselfish. It seeks the best for others—not for us. It's sacrificial. It takes us out of our comfort zones. It prompts us to give up our time, resources, attention, and energy for the sake of someone else, with no thought of repayment. Righteous love is unconditional. It doesn't place demands on people. It isn't given and taken away based on our whims and moods. Righteous love makes a powerful impact because it lets people know that they are worthy of love, just as they are—from us, and from the God we serve.

Compassion goes beyond recognizing that people are hurting or in need. Compassion is that tweaking of our conscience that won't stop until we take their hurt or need personally. Until we involve ourselves in their lives. Until their well-being becomes our well-being. Mere concern is taking a quick look at a problem and saying, "Someone needs to do something about this." Compassion is staring long and hard at a problem and saying, "*I* need to do something about this."

Consideration puts us in other people's shoes. It compels us to examine other people's feelings, perspectives, experiences, and opinions. We may not agree with them, but we need to understand the role these factors play in shaping other people's lives. Being considerate means letting go of the competitive urge to win an argument or humiliate an opponent. A considerate spirit defuses tension and eases combative urges.

There's nothing easy or natural about embracing a spirit of righteous love, compassion, and consideration. But if we journey down this road less traveled, as Johnny Cash encourages, we'll find that we have a surprising number of opportunities to make real differences in other people's lives. We'll also find that we earn the benefit of the doubt in other areas. When people see that we have their best interests in mind, they'll be more likely to listen to us, even when the things we say are hard to hear.

More importantly, if we will commit to pursuing these qualities, we will give people an opportunity to see Christ at work in us. A genuinely loving, compassionate, and considerate attitude toward other people will open doors in ways we can't begin to imagine.

HEAVENLY FATHER, THANK YOU FOR CALLING YOUR PEOPLE TO A HIGHER STANDARD OF LOVE, COMPASSION, AND CONSIDERATION. THANK YOU FOR GIVING ME THE OPPORTUNITY TO STAND APART FROM THE CROWD WHILE AT THE SAME TIME MAKING A DIFFERENCE IN PEOPLE'S LIVES. HELP ME RISE TO THE CHALLENGE. LET YOUR LOVE AND COMPASSION FLOW THROUGH ME. IN JESUS' NAME. AMEN.

COMMON GROUND 43

Christ shed His blood for the weak brother, just as
He did for the greatest, wisest Christian.
—JOHNNY CASH

In Him we have redemption through His blood, the forgiveness of sins,
in accordance with the riches of God's grace that He lavished on us.
—EPHESIANS 1:7–8 NIV

Johnny Cash was born into poverty. He knew what it was like to be an outsider. Yet he also rose to the heights of superstardom. So he also knew what it was like to be an insider. This dual experience, of having been the least and the greatest, gives his quote special gravitas.

When he speaks of the barriers and labels that divide us—"weak," "greatest," wisest"—he does so from a unique perspective. Johnny Cash understood human nature. Especially that part of our nature that feels the need to establish artificial walls. To establish social pecking orders so that we can feel a sense of belonging and superiority. He understood that there can be no "us" without a "them."

Most people have experienced the heady excitement of being an "us," safe and insulated by a like-minded group. As an "us," we celebrate the common bonds we share with others, no matter how tenuous, temporary, or random those bonds may be.

On the flip side, most people have also experienced the loneliness, confusion, and helplessness of being a "them," an outsider for no other reason than the whims of an "us." We know what it is to be the odd person out. The average-looking one ignored by the beautiful crowd. The uncoordinated one among the jocks. The one whose weakness makes it a challenge to interact the way other people do. The one who's not quite as wise or smart as the core group.

Ironically (and cruelly), these experiences of being excluded are what motivate us to seek out cliques of our own, even if it means that other people will experience what we did. And the vicious cycle continues.

The point Johnny Cash makes is that instead of looking for things that divide us, people should look to the things that unite us. After all, the common ground we share is much more important than the artificial boundaries that divide us. That common ground is the grace, forgiveness, and eternal future made possible by the shedding of Christ's blood.

More than that, we should embrace our God-given task to welcome as many people as possible to our common ground. Jesus put it this way to His disciples: "Therefore go and make disciples of all nations, baptizing them in the name of the Father and of the Son and of the Holy Spirit, and teaching them to obey everything I have commanded you" (Matthew 28:19–20 NIV).

We can start to do that by reaching out to the marginalized people in our orbit. By sharing with them the good news that changed our lives. By helping them see the deep connections that join believers and inviting them to experience our fellowship for themselves.

The world is full of dividers. Let's make a name for ourselves as uniters. Let's stake out the ground made possible for us by Christ's sacrifice and invite everyone to join us there.

HEAVENLY FATHER, THANK YOU FOR SENDING YOUR SON, EVEN THOUGH IT MEANT THE SHEDDING OF HIS BLOOD, SO THAT WE CAN HAVE ETERNAL LIFE WITH YOU. THANK YOU FOR GIVING US, IN HIM, A HIGH PRIEST WHO CAN EMPATHIZE WITH OUR FEELINGS OF PAIN AND REJECTION. PLEASE GIVE ME THE COURAGE TO BREAK DOWN ARTIFICIAL BARRIERS AND ESTABLISH BONDS THAT WILL LAST FOR ETERNITY. IN JESUS' NAME. AMEN.

TO WHOM MUCH IS GIVEN

The strong must care for and support the weak.
—JOHNNY CASH

"Everyone to whom much was given, of him much will be required, and from him to whom they entrusted much, they will demand the more."
—LUKE 12:48 ESV

Being strong is a gift from God—and not one to be taken lightly. With His gift comes great responsibility. God doesn't give us strength so that we can enjoy the perks of being strong. He gives us strength to help those who are struggling to find their own strength. Drawing on the principle of Jesus' words in Luke 12, God requires much from those to whom He has given ample strength.

In speaking about what it is that God requires, Johnny Cash chose his words carefully. There's a difference between caring *about* someone and caring *for* someone. In this context, to care *about* someone is to have a good thought, or perhaps a twinge of compassion, for a person who's struggling.

Look at the story of Jesus and His disciples in John 9. As they were walking in Jerusalem, the disciples pointed out a man who had been blind since birth. "Rabbi," they said to Jesus, "who sinned, this man or his parents, that he was born blind?" (verse 2 NIV).

The disciples cared *about* the man, albeit in an abstract, theoretical way. He was a curiosity to them. A there-but-for-the-grace-of-God-go-I reminder to be thankful for their own health. They recognized the blind man's struggle long enough to make a theological teaching moment out of it. But they didn't slow their pace for the man. If pressed, they might have said, "Our thoughts and prayers go out to the blind man and his family." That's caring *about* someone.

But that's not what Johnny Cash was talking about. He didn't use the word *about;* he used the word *for.* Jesus cared *for* the blind man. He wasn't thinking about the theological or social implications of the man's condition. The man's struggle wasn't an abstract concept to Him. Jesus saw the man's need for help and stopped in His tracks to do something about it. He literally got His hands dirty involving Himself in the man's life.

And in doing so, He left us a legacy to live up to.

So how do we support someone who's weak or struggling in the way Jesus did when we don't have His healing power? First, we approach our responsibility with a God-honoring attitude. We rid ourselves of feelings of pity or obligation. Second, we recognize struggling people for who they are. We acknowledge their strengths as well as their weakness. Third, we think in terms of crutches for someone with a broken leg or a guide dog for someone who's legally blind. We find ways to assist people that allow them to maximize their own strength. We give them a support system, someone to lean on when they need it.

In that sense, it's not so much a strong person helping a weak one so much as it is two people with varying degrees of strength working together to create something truly powerful.

HEAVENLY FATHER, THANK YOU FOR THE STRENGTH YOU'VE GIVEN ME. THANK YOU FOR THE PEOPLE YOU'VE BROUGHT INTO MY LIFE TO CARE FOR AND SUPPORT ME WHEN MY STRENGTH FALTERED. THANK YOU ALSO FOR BRINGING PEOPLE INTO MY LIFE WHO I CAN HELP. OPEN MY EYES TO THE NEEDS OF THE PEOPLE AROUND ME. SHOW ME HOW I CAN USE THE STRENGTH YOU'VE GIVEN ME TO MAKE THEIR LIVES BETTER AND TO HELP THEM RECOGNIZE YOUR AMAZING LOVE FOR THEM. IN JESUS' NAME. AMEN.

STANDING ON THE PROMISES

The Scriptures contain truth by divine revelation. Their promises strengthen our faith and give us an anchor.
—Johnny Cash

Above all, you must understand that no prophecy of Scripture came about by the prophet's own interpretation of things. For prophecy never had its origin in the human will, but prophets, though human, spoke from God as they were carried along by the Holy Spirit.
—II Peter 1:20–21 niv

In his own succinct way, Johnny Cash drives home the point that we cannot treat the Bible as just another book. God doesn't give us that option. If the Bible is what it claims to be—if it is what Johnny Cash believed it to be—we can't treat it as merely a source of information. Or merely a source of encouragement. Or merely a source of guidance.

The words "divine revelation" place it in a whole different light. The apostle Peter understood their importance. His point is that no writer of the Bible took pen in hand because he had something he wanted to say. Each one wrote in his own words the message God gave him, all the while guided by the Holy Spirit.

The apostle Paul said, "All Scripture is breathed out by God" (II Timothy 3:16 esv). That means the words in our Bible are the words of our Creator. Scripture is His complete message to us. His guide to pleasing Him. His instruction manual for making life work in the way He intended. His treasure map to ultimate joy and fulfillment.

If the Bible is all those things—if it can be trusted—then, practically speaking, there is nothing more important in this world.

The question is, *can* it be trusted? There's no shortage of objective evidence that points to a hard yes. Consider the unity of Scripture. The Bible was written by at least forty different people, from markedly different backgrounds, over a period of fifteen hundred years or more, in countless different regions. Yet it connects like the pieces of a puzzle to form the Greatest Story Ever Told. There is no other plausible explanation for the Bible's unity than its truthfulness.

Archaeological evidence also supports the Bible's truthfulness. No archaeological discovery has ever proved the Bible to be wrong. In fact, there have been several cases where archaeological scholars questioned the truthfulness of certain historical references in Scripture, only to have those references confirmed by later discoveries.

There's also no shortage of subjective evidence that suggests the Bible is what it claims to be. Billions of lives have been changed by its message. It has guided some of the most important figures in world history. Its message has led people to put an end to slavery, found universities and hospitals, and organize worldwide charities. The words of Scripture impact the way we see the world and each other. In other words, something happens inside of us when we read it regularly and put its words into action.

The Bible is God's Word, and God cannot lie. So we can take His Word as truth. We can put our faith in it. We can build our lives on its promises. We can cling to it when the storms of life blow.

HEAVENLY FATHER, THANK YOU FOR THE TRUSTWORTHINESS OF YOUR WORD. THANK YOU FOR MAKING SURE THAT WE HAVE A SOURCE OF TRUTH AND DIRECTION, SOMETHING SOLID TO HOLD ON TO WHEN LIFE GETS DIFFICULT. OPEN MY EYES TO THE WISDOM OF YOUR WORD. SHOW ME HOW I CAN APPLY ITS TRUTH TO MY DAILY LIFE. IN JESUS' NAME. AMEN.

EVER HOPEFUL

*God is our hope, and in Him we do hope. God is our joy and our
peace. His blessings are for filling ourselves with His joy.*
—Johnny Cash

*"If we are thrown into the blazing furnace, the God we serve is able to
deliver us from it, and He will deliver us from Your Majesty's hand. But
even if He does not, we want you to know, Your Majesty, that we will
not serve your gods or worship the image of gold you have set up."*
—Daniel 3:17–18 niv

How often do you use the word *hope* in a typical day? "I hope it doesn't rain." "I hope the Cubs win." "I hope we have enough gas to get home." We put our hope in a lot of different things, most of which we can't control.

That powerlessness isn't a problem if the consequences are no greater than a few afternoon showers or another Cubs heartbreaker. But this issue of hope goes much deeper than that. Right now, there are parents starting to realize that, despite their best efforts, they can't keep their kids safe and protected forever. There are single adults starting to wonder if they'll ever meet the right person. There are once-healthy people facing devastating medical crises. In these cases, powerlessness can be terrifying.

They, and we, need something solid to put our hope in. Something trustworthy. Something powerful.

We need God.

Time and again the Lord has proved Himself worthy of our hope. Not because He removes obstacles and challenges from our lives, but because He shepherds us through them. The book of Daniel tells the story of Shadrach, Meshach, and Abednego, three men who placed their hope in God in a remarkable way. The three were given a choice: bow down and worship an idol or get thrown in a fiery furnace. They knew God's command against worshiping idols, so they refused to bow down. And since they were powerless to change the consequences of their refusal, they handed their impending fiery death to God.

But here's what we need to understand about their experience: they didn't put their hope in God because they were certain that He was going to rescue them. Look at that passage from Daniel 3 again. They were certain that God *could* rescue, if He chose to. They just weren't sure what His choice would be.

But it didn't matter anyway. Their hope was in God. Wherever He led, they were prepared to go. Whatever He had in store for them, they were prepared to endure. That's what it means to place our hope in God: to realize that His will, whatever it may be, is the best possible course of action.

What's in it for us? Joy and peace. Look at the apostle Paul's words in Philippians 4:4–7 NIV: "Rejoice in the Lord always. I will say it again: Rejoice! . . . Do not be anxious about anything, but in every situation, by prayer and petition, with thanksgiving, present your requests to God. And the peace of God, which transcends all understanding, will guard your hearts and your minds in Christ Jesus."

When we let go of our anxiety and put our trust in God by turning every situation over to Him, we will find joy and peace that we can't explain. That's God's promise to us.

HEAVENLY FATHER, THANK YOU FOR BEING THE SOURCE OF MY HOPE. THANK YOU FOR PROVING YOURSELF RELIABLE OVER AND OVER AGAIN. CREATE IN ME THE SPIRIT AND CONFIDENCE THAT ALLOWED SHADRACH, MESHACH, AND ABEDNEGO TO STEP INTO THE FIERY FURNACE WITH THEIR HOPE UNDIMINISHED. LET ME SHOW OTHERS WHAT HOPE IN YOU LOOKS LIKE. IN JESUS' NAME. AMEN.

MANY MEMBERS, ONE BODY

*In the power of the Holy Ghost we realize our union and
communion with Christ and our fellow Christians.*
—Johnny Cash

*For just as the body is one and has many members,
and all the members of the body, though many,
are one body, so it is with Christ.*
—I Corinthians 12:12 ESV

The power of the Holy Spirit makes the Christian life possible. It energizes every aspect of our walk with Christ. Yet we will never experience the full potential of the Holy Spirit's power unless we are connected to the people of God through the church.

After all, as believers, we are all members of Christ's body. Without the connection to the rest of the body, we are like severed limbs. Spiritually speaking, we quickly wither and die.

One of the most inspiring examples of what the Holy Spirit can accomplish in and through the church is found in Acts 2:42–47. Referring to the congregation of believers in Jerusalem, Luke—the author of the book of Acts—says, "They were continually devoting themselves to the apostles' teaching and to fellowship, to the breaking of bread and to prayer. Everyone kept feeling a sense of awe; and many wonders and signs were taking place through the apostles. And all the believers were together and had all things in common. . . . Day by day continuing with one mind in the temple, and breaking bread from house to house, they were taking their meals together with gladness and sincerity of heart, praising God and having favor with all the people" (NASB).

And when the union and communion between believers is this strong, look at what happens: "And the Lord was adding to their number day by day those who were being saved" (verse 47 NASB).

The writer of Hebrews helps us understand what happens when fellowship is a priority. "And let's consider how to encourage one another in love and good deeds, not abandoning our own meeting together, as is the habit of some people, but encouraging one another; and all the more as you see the day drawing near" (Hebrews 10:24–25 NASB). When believers get together, we have an opportunity to produce something good in one another. We have an opportunity to spur one another to love and to do good deeds.

The church is also where our spiritual gifts—which are given by the Holy Spirit—prove especially valuable. Sometimes in ways that are obvious, sometimes in ways that are less so.

Within the church, God puts us in contact with other Christians who have gifts that we don't have. So we have an opportunity to observe and learn from them how to exercise those gifts. For example, God calls us to be generous. He wants us to give liberally of our personal resources. So He puts us in contact with believers in the church who have the gift of giving. Their example can serve as an inspiration and encouragement to us to be more giving.

Likewise, God wants us to be merciful. So He puts us in contact with believers who have the gift of mercy. Through their example, we learn to identify with and comfort those who are in distress.

The more we embrace our union and communion with fellow believers in the church, the more we unleash the power of the Holy Spirit in our lives.

> **HEAVENLY FATHER, THANK YOU FOR GIVING ME YOUR HOLY SPIRIT TO GUIDE AND ENERGIZE MY WALK WITH CHRIST. HELP ME MAKE A DIFFERENCE IN THE LIVES OF OTHERS AS THEY CONTINUE TO MAKE A DIFFERENCE IN MINE. IN JESUS' NAME. AMEN.**

A WORTHY AMBITION

Our ambition should be to be acceptable to the Lord; to be simple, quiet, and consistent in ordinary Christian living.
—Johnny Cash

On the contrary, we speak as those approved by God to be entrusted with the gospel. We are not trying to please people but God, who tests our hearts.
—I Thessalonians 2:4 niv

What do you want to be? The question is an invitation to reveal our deepest ambitions. *I want to be a senior-level manager in five years. I want to be a better parent. I want to be thirty pounds lighter before my high-school reunion.* But how many of us think in terms of our spiritual ambition?

And what *should* be our spiritual ambition? To win one hundred souls for Christ? To read through the Bible in a year? To become the most popular Sunday school teacher in the whole church?

Johnny Cash encourages us to aim higher, although it may not seem that way at first glance at his words. The three attitudes he calls us to seem as though they would come naturally to us. Or at the very least require a minimum amount of work. What could be easier than walking with Christ simply, quietly, and consistently? Look a little closer, though, and you'll see that there's no naivete in Johnny Cash's words. He understood well the challenge at the heart of his words.

Leading a simple Christian life is challenging because our impulse is to make things as complicated as possible. We filter the truth of God's message through our own preferences and prejudices. Jesus said, "Love your enemies." Our first instinct is to draw up a list of exceptions and then try to narrow the definition of what constitutes "love." The Bible says, "Flee immorality." We invite it for an extended stay and then wonder why we can't shake certain destructive habits. The simple approach to the Christian life is to find out exactly what the Lord wants from us—through prayer, Bible study, and time spent worshiping Him—and then do it to the utmost of our ability.

Leading a quiet Christian life is challenging because our culture rewards attention-getting self-promotion. When it comes to service, "Do not let your left hand know what your right hand is doing" has given way to "Do not forget to post pictures of or thoughts about your service on social media." The feedback that comes from going public with our private relationship with Christ can be intoxicating. It can also distract us from our true purpose, which is to focus our attention on the Lord.

Leading a consistent Christian life is challenging because at any given moment we have dozens, maybe even hundreds, of things looking to replace prayer, Bible study, and worship on our priority list. Most of those options have more surface appeal than our Christian responsibilities. They promise more fun and less work.

The key to "ordinary Christian living," as Johnny Cash puts it, is discipline. We can learn not to complicate our simple faith. We can learn not to invite noise into our quiet faith. We can learn not to get distracted from our consistent faith. The Holy Spirit stands ready to help us discover how extraordinary our ordinary faith can be.

HEAVENLY FATHER, THANK YOU FOR MAKING ME ACCEPTABLE IN YOUR SIGHT THROUGH THE SACRIFICE OF YOUR SON. THANK YOU FOR THE OPPORTUNITY TO GROW CLOSER TO YOU. GIVE ME THE INSIGHT TO RECOGNIZE WHERE I FALL SHORT AND THE DISCIPLINE TO MAINTAIN A SIMPLE, QUIET, AND CONSISTENT RELATIONSHIP WITH YOU. IN JESUS' NAME. AMEN.

LOOKING FOR ANSWERS

God always answers prayer, always in His own way. Sometimes
He answers in a way we don't ask, but He always answers.

—JOHNNY CASH

"If you abide in me, and my words abide in you, ask
whatever you wish, and it will be done for you."

—JOHN 15:7 ESV

Johnny Cash taps into a concern that most believers experience at some point in our walk with Christ: that our prayers don't seem to go any higher than the ceiling. We look around at the situations that we've asked God to change and find them distressingly unchanged. So we have a tendency to assume the worst. About God. About our relationship with Him. About the effectiveness of prayer.

Before we jump to any conclusions, however, we need to understand a few things about prayer. First, our prayers reflect our priorities. Every time we pray, we enter the presence of the Creator of the universe. We have an opportunity to express our awe of Him, our appreciation of His perfections, and our thankfulness to Him in a one-on-one setting. That's huge. Much bigger than any request we may have of Him. If we want to maximize the impact of our prayers, we need to prioritize the time we spend praising God.

Second, our prayers reflect our spiritual maturity. If we skip past the first half of Jesus' words in John 15:7, we may be tempted to treat prayer as a blank check. We see the words "ask whatever you wish" and start making our wish list. In contrast, mature believers base their approach to prayer on Jesus' words in the first half of the verse: "If you abide in me, and my words abide in you." He's talking about a soul-deep understanding of, and desire to obey, God and

His Word. The deeper we dive into God's Word and the more time we spend in His presence through prayer and quiet time, the better our understanding is of His will. The better we understand His will, the more likely we are to pray for it to be accomplished, instead of praying for our own selfish desires.

Third, our perspective is limited. Life, to us, is like trying to make our way through a giant hedge maze. We can't see what's around the next turn. God, on the other hand, can see the entire maze from an overhead view. He can see where every path leads. He knows which route will lead us where we're supposed to go and which routes will lead to dead ends. If we stubbornly insist on telling God where He should lead us, we're not going to make much progress.

Fourth, unanswered prayers—or prayers that *seem* to go unanswered—are some of the greatest blessings we'll ever receive. God, in His patience, listens to our requests over and over. In II Corinthians 12, the apostle Paul talks about a physical ailment that he refers to as his "thorn" in his "flesh." Three times he asks God to remove it from him, and three times God opts not to. He has a much better plan that involves Paul's ailment. And so it is with our prayers. God, in His wisdom, chooses not to give us what we ask for. Instead, He gives us something unimaginably better.

> FATHER, THANK YOU FOR THE PRIVILEGE OF YOUR COMPANY. LET ME NEVER LOSE MY SENSE OF HUMILITY AND AWE WHEN I COME TO YOU IN PRAYER. HELP ME SEE THE BIG PICTURE SO THAT MY REQUESTS WILL ALIGN WITH YOUR WILL. GIVE ME THE PEACE OF MIND TO RECOGNIZE THAT YOUR ANSWER IS ALWAYS WHAT'S BEST FOR ME. IN JESUS' NAME. AMEN.

A SHOW OF APPRECIATION

A show of loving appreciation is different from flattery. Christian courtesy and praise from a fellow Christian is itself a very good testimony of our faith in the Lord.
—Johnny Cash

Do not withhold good from those to whom it is due, when it is in your power to do it.
—Proverbs 3:27 ESV

As a student of Scripture, Johnny Cash understood the surface appeal of flattery. He also understood its drawbacks and dangers. The first drawback is that flattery is often insincere. It focuses on surface-y things—things that require no effort or time to recognize. Flattery also usually has an agenda. Some people offer it to call attention to themselves—to make sure that others recognize their kindness and impeccable character. Other people use flattery as a prelude to asking for a favor or trying to manipulate someone in some way.

Flattery is dangerous to those who fall for it. When they finally recognize it for what it is, they lose a little self-confidence. They don't know who to trust, so they build emotional barriers to keep other people from manipulating them. They're left feeling used and cynical about others.

Sincere praise, on the other hand, can be life-changing—in the best possible sense. A show of loving appreciation can transform the way people look at themselves. It can open their eyes to possibilities they never imagined before. This is especially true for people who aren't used to hearing positive things about themselves.

Think of the most meaningful word of praise you ever got from someone. What made it so special? What did it do for your self-image? What impact did it have on your life?

Johnny Cash suggests that a show of loving appreciation for someone else is an outflow of God's love for us. It's also strong evidence of our relationship with Him. He pours into us so that we can pour into others.

Sincere praise goes beyond the surface. It says to the person, "I see something meaningful inside you—something substantial that could make a godly difference in other people's lives." A show of loving appreciation can help people recognize their God-given gifts and give them direction in how to put those gifts to use.

Sincere praise has no agenda other than speaking truth to people in a way that builds them up. But it must absolutely start with the truth. Telling people what we think they want to hear, when it's not necessarily true, does no one any good. God doesn't want us to mislead one another. He wants us to take the time and effort to recognize the good in others—the unique abilities He wove into our skill sets.

Sincere praise doesn't come natural to everyone. It's something we have to work at. We must train ourselves to look for opportunities to offer sincere praise in our daily lives. We'll find those opportunities everywhere. So we also need the courage and creativity to voice our praise in a memorable way.

Johnny Cash underscores the most important effect of sincere praise: bringing glory to the God we serve. The kind of courtesy and praise Johnny Cash calls believers to is rare in our world. When people see and hear it, they pay attention. They're drawn to it, as well as to the One who inspires it.

> HEAVENLY FATHER, THANK YOU FOR THE PEOPLE IN MY LIFE WHO MODELED LOVING APPRECIATION AND CHRISTIAN PRAISE. LET ME LEARN FROM THEIR EXAMPLE SO THAT I CAN MAKE A DIFFERENCE IN OTHER PEOPLE'S LIVES. GIVE ME THE DISCERNMENT TO RECOGNIZE FLATTERY FOR WHAT IT IS. GIVE ME THE WISDOM TO KNOW HOW TO PRAISE PEOPLE IN A WAY THAT WILL MAKE A DIFFERENCE IN THEIR LIVES. IN JESUS' NAME. AMEN.

BEYOND HOPE

No Christian should regard any sinner as a hopeless case.
—JOHNNY CASH

"If a man has a hundred sheep and one of them wanders away, what will he do? Won't he leave the ninety-nine others on the hills and go out to search for the one that is lost? And if he finds it, I tell you the truth, he will rejoice over it more than over the ninety-nine that didn't wander away! In the same way, it is not my heavenly Father's will that even one of these little ones should perish."
—MATTHEW 18:12–14 NLT

Johnny Cash's words hit home with a lot of people—but for different reasons. Some people see their friends or loved ones in his words. They know all too well the agony of waiting, worrying, hoping, and praying that someone dear to them would recognize and change their self-destructive ways. They know what it is to reach the point where they've been disappointed and hurt so many times that they just can't work up any more empathy. They've resigned themselves to a worst-case scenario.

Other people see themselves in Johnny Cash's words. They know what it is to be called a hopeless case. Perhaps they've even thought of themselves in such terms. But what if they manage to prove everyone, including themselves, wrong? What if they successfully battle their demons? What if their story has a happy ending? Who will share their victory? Who will they remember as being blessings in their lives? The people who refused to see them as hopeless cases.

Jesus' words in Matthew 18 assure us that the Lord does not see hopeless cases. The one stray sheep easily could have been written off as an acceptable loss. The Shepherd had a 99 percent success rate. How much could the one-hundredth sheep possibly matter? Quite a bit, as it turns out. The Shepherd dropped everything to bring back the lost sheep. He refused to see the situation as hopeless. He saw potential where few others would have.

What would happen if we took the same approach to the "hopeless" people in our lives? To do that, we need to follow Jesus' lead in three ways. First, we need to look past current circumstances. No matter how bleak a situation looks, God can change it. We can't write off someone as being hopeless without denying God's ability to work in that person's life. There is no wisdom in underestimating God's power to change current circumstances.

Second, we need to put aside our personal feelings. The Shepherd didn't punish the lost sheep for his wandering. He didn't try to shame him by comparing him to the other ninety-nine. We can't deny the pain and disappointment we feel when people we care about make destructive life choices. But we also can't let those emotions keep us from pursuing them like the Shepherd did the lost sheep.

Third, we need to rejoice when the situation calls for it. The Lord's work in someone's life is always cause for celebration. Our rejoicing helps ease tension during the lost sheep's return to the fold. It also draws the attention of others who may be feeling lost and in need of a Shepherd.

> HEAVENLY FATHER, THANK YOU FOR NOT GIVING UP ON ME. THANK YOU FOR LOOKING PAST MY FLAWS AND SEEING THE POTENTIAL WITHIN. MAKE ME AN INSTRUMENT OF YOUR GRACE IN OTHER PEOPLE'S LIVES. GIVE ME THE PATIENCE AND PERSPECTIVE TO SEE HOPE WHERE OTHERS SEE HOPELESSNESS. HELP ME MAKE A DIFFERENCE IN THE LIVES OF PEOPLE WHO ARE STRUGGLING. IN JESUS' NAME. AMEN.

Let us then with confidence draw near to the throne of grace, that we may receive mercy and find grace to help in time of need.

—Hebrews 4:16 esv

WILL WORK FOR GOD

We work for God because we love Him and we
want to, not because we are forced to.
—JOHNNY CASH

Whatever you do, work heartily, as for the Lord
and not for men, knowing that from the Lord
you will receive the inheritance as your reward.
You are serving the Lord Christ.
—COLOSSIANS 3:23–24 ESV

Johnny Cash was no stranger to hard work. He recognized work for the blessing it is—in his music and in his walk with Christ. Our ability to work, and our *responsibility* to work, lies at the core of our being. Look at the creation account in Genesis 2. God created man (verse 7). Then God planted the garden of Eden (verses 8–14). "The LORD God took the man and put him in the garden of Eden to work it and keep it" (verse 15 ESV).

No sooner had God's Spirit filled our nostrils with our first breath than we had a job to do. A work ethic is hardwired into our system. Remember, too, that this was before sin ruined everything. This was God's original, perfect plan for humankind. He designed us to find fulfillment in our work.

Johnny Cash alludes to the truth that our work should reflect our Creator. Our work ethic isn't tied to paychecks, good reviews, or job satisfaction. Our work gives us the opportunity to draw attention to the God we serve. When we do our work with integrity—giving our best effort, being supportive of the people we work with, going above and beyond our responsibilities—we earn the respect of our coworkers and managers. We also create an opportunity to talk to them about what makes us different.

One of the more amazing aspects of working to honor God is seeing what He can do with what we do. God blesses our efforts by magnifying them in ways we can't imagine. Think of the boy who carried a basket of loaves and fish to the remote area where Jesus had retreated. The Lord magnified his work by feeding five thousand people with his meager provisions. The young man had no idea that his work of lugging the food a considerable distance would yield such dramatic results. The same goes for our work. Every job we perform with a sense of integrity and a desire to honor God is like a pebble dropped into a still pond. We have no idea how far the ripples will extend. When we approach our work the right way, we offer a powerful testimony.

The sense of fulfillment that comes from finishing our work is God's gift to us. Doing quality work makes us feel essential and productive. When our work involves our spiritual gifts—the unique talents and abilities given to us by God's Holy Spirit—our feelings of fulfillment are magnified. And because our work pleases God, it strengthens our relationship with Him.

Still, God offers even more incentive to would-be workers. In Matthew 25, Jesus shares a parable about three servants. The first two servants work hard to maximize what has been given to them for the sake of their master. And their master says to each of them, "Well done, my good and faithful servant. . . . Let's celebrate together!" (verses 21, 23 NLT). The same celebration awaits us, if we pursue a godly attitude toward work.

> **HEAVENLY FATHER, THANK YOU FOR CREATING US WITH A PURPOSE. THANK YOU FOR HELPING US FIND MEANING IN WORK. HELP ME MAINTAIN AN ATTITUDE TOWARD WORK THAT HONORS YOU. GIVE ME THE WISDOM TO RECOGNIZE WORK THAT IS WORTH MY TIME AND ENERGY. IN JESUS' NAME. AMEN.**

AMAZING GRACE

I am saved by God's grace. I am fortunate to be one of His chosen.
—Johnny Cash

For by grace you have been saved through faith.
And this is not your own doing; it is the gift of God,
not a result of works, so that no one may boast.
—Ephesians 2:8–9 esv

Few people experience the kind of depravity that John Newton experienced. Born in London in 1725, he lost his mother when he was six years old. His father, a ship's captain, took young John to sea when he was eleven. In time, John got a job as a crewman on a slave ship. His crewmates left him stranded in West Africa, where he became a slave himself. Eventually he was rescued, but on the journey home, his ship almost sank. John prayed to God, and the vessel reached port safely. Shortly thereafter, Newton became a Christian.

Unfortunately, his life didn't change right away. He became the captain of a slave ship and sold hundreds of people into slavery. He destroyed lives and families. The full weight of his actions didn't hit him until several years later. Burdened by the guilt of his actions and stunned by God's mercy toward him, John Newton poured out his feelings in the lyrics of "Amazing Grace."

Almost two hundred and fifty years later, God's grace continues to amaze. Grace is God's undeserved favor toward us. We've done nothing to earn it, yet He gives it generously. What we can do is respond to His grace in a way that honors Him.

First, we can put our faith in it. Look at the words of Paul in Ephesians 2:8–9 again. If we embrace that truth, we will not rely on our own good works, knowledge, or personal principles. Instead, we will constantly acknowledge that only God's grace makes it possible for us to be saved.

Second, we can refuse to misuse God's grace. Some people say that His grace gives us freedom to sin. After all, we will be forgiven. But that misses the point completely. As Paul says in Romans 6:1–2, "What shall we say then? Are we to continue in sin that grace may abound? By no means! How can we who died to sin still live in it?" (ESV). God's grace gives us the opportunity to break free from sin. That's how He wants us to use it.

Third, we can allow His grace to transform us. Paul explains how in Titus 2:12. He says God's grace compels us "to renounce ungodliness and worldly passions, and to live self-controlled, upright, and godly lives in the present age" (ESV). He's talking about spiritual growth, which is the natural result of embracing God's grace.

Fourth, we can incorporate grace into our own relationships. This is what Jesus is talking about in John 13:34: "A new commandment I give to you, that you love one another: just as I have loved you, you also are to love one another" (ESV). The grace that God gives us is so overwhelming and so constant that it should spill out of our lives into the lives of others. The loving concern that we show others springs from the loving concern that God shows us.

That's how we help others recognize the sweet sound of amazing grace.

> **HEAVENLY FATHER, THANK YOU FOR THE GRACE THAT YOU SHOW ME EVERY DAY OF MY LIFE. THANK YOU FOR LOVING ME EVEN THOUGH I CAN DO NOTHING TO EARN YOUR LOVE. BLESS MY EFFORTS TO FULLY EMBRACE YOUR GRACE SO THAT I MAY GROW IN MY RELATIONSHIP WITH YOU AND WITH OTHERS. IN JESUS' NAME. AMEN.**

ROCK BOTTOM

There is not a pit so low or so slimy that man wallows in that God will not reach His hand into to pull man out if he will but call on Him.

—Johnny Cash

I waited patiently for the Lord to help me,
and He turned to me and heard my cry.
He lifted me out of the pit of despair,
out of the mud and the mire.
He set my feet on solid ground
and steadied me as I walked along.
He has given me a new song to sing,
a hymn of praise to our God.
Many will see what He has done and be amazed.
They will put their trust in the Lord.

—Psalm 40:1–3 nlt

Johnny Cash understood from personal experience that no one can testify about God's grace like someone who has hit rock bottom. He lived the words of King David in Psalm 40. More importantly, he emerged from the depths and then made it his mission to show others the way out too.

Let's look at this issue of emerging from the depths from two different perspectives. First, let's consider how we can come back from our lowest point. The key to the comeback is to recognize rock bottom for what it is. We must have a moment of realization of how far we've fallen. Look at the story of the prodigal son in Luke 15. The young man demanded his inheritance from his father and lost it all pursuing a life of debauchery. When a famine struck the land where he was living, he took a job feeding pigs. Yet he became so desperate for food that he looked longingly at the pig slop. Unfortunately, even that was off-limits to him. Seeing pigs eat better fare than he ate was the moment of realization for the prodigal son. It was the trigger that set in motion his plan to return to his father.

We may never fall quite so far, but we will experience moments that drive home our spiritual distance from God. These moments may come in the form of a prompting by the Holy Spirit, words of hard truth from a friend, or a decision to no longer deceive ourselves. We need to recognize these moments as wake-up calls and take the first steps in our journey back to God: turning our backs to our sinful lifestyle and reaching out to God.

Second, let's consider how we can help others out of their lowest depths. In I Corinthians 12, the apostle Paul describes believers as the body of Christ. Every believer is part of that body. Together we accomplish the Lord's work in this world. So when someone who is in a slimy pit reaches out to God, ours may be the hand he or she grabs.

God gives us the privilege of sharing His love with the people who need it most. We reach out to people at their lowest points by noticing them on the street. By engaging them in conversation. By offering them encouragement and support. By taking the necessary steps to meet their needs. By helping them understand that they matter to us.

HEAVENLY FATHER, I PRAISE YOU FOR YOUR REACH. NO ONE IS TOO FAR GONE FOR YOU TO SAVE. THANK YOU FOR CARING ABOUT US EVEN AT OUR LOWEST POINTS. KEEP ME AWARE OF MY ROLE IN THE BODY OF CHRIST. HELP ME RECOGNIZE PEOPLE WHO NEED A HAND. GIVE ME THE COURAGE TO REACH OUT TO THEM AND THE HUMILITY TO GIVE YOU THE PRAISE FOR IT. IN JESUS' NAME. AMEN.

LEARNING THE HARD WAY

You build on failure. You use it as a stepping-stone. Close the door on the past. You don't try to forget the mistakes, but you don't dwell on them. You don't let them have any of your energy or any of your time or any of your space.

—JOHNNY CASH

We can rejoice, too, when we run into problems and trials, for we know that they help us develop endurance. And endurance develops strength of character, and character strengthens our confident hope of salvation. And this hope will not lead to disappointment. For we know how dearly God loves us, because He has given us the Holy Spirit to fill our hearts with His love.

—ROMANS 5:3–5 NLT

It's no surprise that an artist who took the kind of chances in his work that Johnny Cash took—and who struggled with the kind of temptations that he struggled with—would develop an insightful, lived-in perspective on failure. Yet Johnny Cash's life was one of forward momentum. He refused to allow his failures to define him or to stop him.

If we're going to learn from his example, we need to do four things when we fail. First, we need to own our failure. It's tempting to make excuses or blame someone else, but if we're going to learn everything God has to teach us, we need to be honest with Him and with ourselves. We need to be able to admit, "This is on me. I did something wrong." This is especially important if our failure affects our relationship with God. We need to confess what we've done and ask for His forgiveness. The same goes for failures that affect other people. We must take full responsibility, as well as the necessary steps to restore our relationship.

Second, we need to understand our failure. We do that by asking God to help us recognize decisions along the way that might have led to it. We need to answer honestly some difficult questions. Were we trying to do too much? Did we ignore any warning signs? Did we put ourselves in the wrong place at the wrong time? Were we influenced by someone else? Were we too susceptible to temptation? The point here is not to dwell on or obsess over our failure, but to learn what we can from it to keep from making the same mistake again.

Third, we need to put our failure in perspective. We need to recognize that our failure does not define us. Many heroes of the faith failed miserably at some point in their lives. Moses killed a man. Peter denied knowing Jesus on three separate occasions. Paul helped persecute Christians. Yet all were later used by God in powerful ways. We can find inspiration in their stories, motivation to learn from and then move past our failures to find what God has in store for us.

Fourth, we need to grow from our failure. One thing failure can do is make us empathetic to other people who have failed or who are struggling. We can become instruments of God's grace in their lives. We can help them learn to forgive themselves and regain their momentum. We can turn our own failure into something positive for others.

> HEAVENLY FATHER, THANK YOU FOR REFUSING TO GIVE UP ON ME, NO MATTER HOW MANY TIMES I FAIL. THANK YOU FOR THE OPPORTUNITY TO LEARN AND GROW FROM MY FAILURES. HELP ME KEEP A HEALTHY PERSPECTIVE ON THE TIMES I FALL SHORT SO THAT I CAN RESTORE MY RELATIONSHIP WITH YOU, WITH OTHERS, AND WITH MYSELF. IN JESUS' NAME. AMEN.

WRESTLING WITH THE ALMIGHTY

My arms are too short to box with God.
—Johnny Cash

Then the man said, "Your name will no longer be Jacob, but Israel, because you have struggled with God and with humans and have overcome."
—Genesis 32:28 NIV

Johnny Cash learned early on what many people take years to understand: God is undefeated. He can't be beaten, overcome, or outsmarted. He can't be convinced by our arguments or moved by our excuses. Yet that doesn't stop us from challenging Him from time to time.

We may even feel justified in doing it. After all, submitting to God's will can be hard, especially when it becomes clear that God isn't taking into account our comfort, convenience, or preferences. So we dig in our heels. We ignore the promptings of the Holy Spirit, hoping that He will change His mind or give up. We allow our relationship with our heavenly Father to grow distant while we sulk. Occasionally we vent our frustrations or anger in a direct manner. And we join an illustrious roster of people who have gone into battle against God.

Genesis 32 tells one such story. Jacob was on his way to meet Esau, the brother he had swindled years earlier. For all Jacob knew, Esau was about to exact his revenge. Jacob sent his family ahead and spent the night by himself, camped by a river. Perhaps he used his time alone to take stock of his life, the way he pursued his own desires, always ready with a scam or lie to help him get away.

Suddenly a mysterious figure appeared, and Jacob started wrestling with him. The two engaged in real physical combat all night. Eventually the mysterious figure dislocated Jacob's hip, so that he became nearly helpless. Realizing that he had been wrestling with God, Jacob asked for a blessing.

The wrestling match, and Jacob's injury from it, ensured that he would approach his meeting with Esau in a spirit of humility. That likely would explain why the reunion turned out to be more successful and blessed than Jacob could have imagined. Jacob wrestled with God and lost. And won.

The short book of Jonah tells another wrestling story. God instructed his prophet Jonah to go to Nineveh to preach. But that was the last thing Jonah wanted to do. Jonah hated the Ninevites. He wanted them to face God's wrath. So he booked passage on a ship headed in the opposite direction. He defied God and then tried to run from Him. We all know how that turned out. From the belly of a fish, Jonah had time to contemplate the fruitlessness of his battle. He wrestled with God and lost. And Nineveh won.

Jacob and Jonah would both attest to the truth that Johnny Cash spoke. Wrestling with God is a waste of our time and energy. In the end, God's will *will* be done, no matter how hard we fight it.

Obedience is the better strategy. When we obey, we are acknowledging not only that God's will is inevitable, but also that it will prove to be the best thing for everyone involved—including us—in the end. We were created to obey and serve God. When we do, we find the kind of peace and fulfillment that nothing else can bring.

> **HEAVENLY FATHER, THANK YOU FOR ALWAYS HAVING MY BEST INTERESTS AT HEART. THANK YOU FOR BEING PATIENT WITH ME WHEN I FAIL TO RECOGNIZE THAT TRUTH. WRESTLE WITH ME FOR AS LONG AS IT TAKES FOR ME TO EMBRACE YOUR WILL. IN JESUS' NAME. AMEN.**

A HOLE IN YOUR HEART

There's no way around grief and loss: you can dodge all you want, but sooner or later you just have to go into it, through it, and, hopefully, come out the other side. The world you find there will never be the same as the world you left.

—JOHNNY CASH

The LORD is near to the brokenhearted and saves those who are crushed in spirit.

—PSALM 34:18 NASB

Someone once said that you never really recover from the loss of a loved one; you just eventually learn to go through the motions of your old life in a convincing way. That statement, combined with the quote from Johnny Cash, reveals the emotional devastation that lies at the heart of grief. As Johnny Cash's use of the word "hopefully" suggests, not everyone emerges from the other side.

The Word of God has much to say on the topic, which should come as no surprise. Jesus grieved the death of His friend Lazarus in John 11, even though He knew He was going to raise Lazarus from the dead. God Himself is certainly no stranger to grief. His plan of salvation required the death of His only Son.

So if we're going to find a way through our own grief, the best place to turn is to the pages of Scripture. The words of the psalmist quoted above emphasize that grief need never be a solo experience. Psalm 23 points out that God walks with us through the valley of the shadow of death. Even though we may not always sense His nearness, He maintains a constant watch over us.

Jesus assured His followers that grief will not get the final word. "Blessed are you who are hungry now, for you shall be satisfied. Blessed are you who weep now, for you shall laugh." (Luke 6:21 ESV). Though we may not believe it possible in the depths of our sadness, we will feel joy again. That's a promise to cling to when we're in distress. We must let time take its healing course.

In his vision of heaven, the apostle John reveals an even more hopeful promise: "He will wipe every tear from their eyes, and there will be no more death or sorrow or crying or pain. All these things are gone forever" (Revelation 21:4 NLT). In heaven, we will experience no grief, pain, or sorrow, because there will be no death. Everything sad will fall away, and we'll be left with God's unending love.

In the meantime, we can use our own experiences with grief—and God's healing—as we reach out to others who are struggling. As Paul put it in II Corinthians 1:3–4: "Blessed be the God and Father of our Lord Jesus Christ, the Father of mercies and God of all comfort, who comforts us in all our affliction, so that we may be able to comfort those who are in any affliction, with the comfort with which we ourselves are comforted by God" (ESV).

God comforts us in our darkest times and gives us strength to endure so that we can give comfort and strength to others during their worst times. As we emerge from our season of grief, we can look to God as an example of how to provide comfort and love to others during their seasons of grief.

> **HEAVENLY FATHER, THANK YOU FOR THE PEOPLE WHO HAVE IMPACTED MY LIFE. THANK YOU FOR THE OPPORTUNITY TO LOVE AND BE LOVED BY THOSE WHO ARE NO LONGER WITH ME. HELP ME FIND HEALING IN THE MIDST OF MY GRIEF. GIVE ME THE STRENGTH AND ENCOURAGEMENT TO LIVE MY LIFE IN A WAY THAT HONORS THEIR MEMORY AND PLEASES YOU. IN JESUS' NAME. AMEN.**

YOU CAN'T SPELL COMPASSION WITHOUT P-A-I-N

Follow your heart. That's what I do. Compassion is something I
have a lot of, because I've been through a lot of pain in my life.
Anybody who has suffered a lot of pain has a lot of compassion.
—JOHNNY CASH

The LORD is gracious and compassionate, slow to anger and rich in love.
The LORD is good to all; He has compassion on all He has made.
—PSALM 145:8–9 NIV

Johnny Cash's words resonate because they get to the heart of our Christian faith. All believers are called to a life of Christlikeness, and compassion is one of the key ingredients of Christlikeness.

Jesus' life was marked by compassion. The motivation for many of His miracles was His deep concern for the suffering of others.

"And a man with leprosy came to Jesus, imploring Him and kneeling down, and saying to Him, 'If You are willing, You can make me clean.' Moved with compassion, Jesus reached out with His hand and touched him, and said to him, 'I am willing; be cleansed'" (Mark 1:40–41 NASB).

"Seeing the crowds, He felt compassion for them, because they were distressed and downcast, like sheep without a shepherd" (Matthew 9:36 NASB).

What's more, two of Jesus' best-known parables teach the importance of compassion. In the story of the prodigal son, the father, who represents God, patiently waits for the return of his wayward child. Notice the father's initial reaction after seeing his son: "So he set out and came to his father. But when he was still a long way off, his father saw him and felt compassion for him, and ran and embraced him and kissed him" (Luke 15:20 NASB).

In the parable of the good Samaritan, Jesus contrasted the indifference of the religious leaders toward an injured man with the compassion shown by a foreigner. The Samaritan, unlike the religious leaders of the day, was genuinely concerned with other people's needs. "But a Samaritan who was on a journey came upon him; and when he saw him, he felt compassion, and came to him and bandaged up his wounds, pouring oil and wine on them; and he put him on his own animal, and brought him to an inn and took care of him" (Luke 10:33–34 NASB).

The psalmist, in the passage at the beginning of this devotion, makes it clear that God values and demonstrates compassion. It stands to reason, then, as beings created in His image, that we possess the gift of compassion as well. Like Johnny Cash, we can turn our pain into something valuable. Something that will make a difference in other people's lives. Something that will point them toward God, the source of perfect compassion.

To do that, we first must find healing from our own pain. We can't show others the way if we haven't traveled the path ourselves. Second, we must find the courage to reach out to other hurting people. Third, we must find common ground with them—not because we know exactly what they're going through, but because we traveled similar ground. Fourth, we must find ways to apply the lessons of our own healing to their situation. Fifth, we must pray for God's continued healing in their lives.

FATHER, THANK YOU FOR SHOWING COMPASSION TO ME—FOR REACHING OUT WHEN I STRUGGLED, FOR ENCOURAGING ME WHEN DISCOURAGEMENT THREATENED TO IMMOBILIZE ME, FOR GIVING ME A SENSE OF PURPOSE WHEN I COULD FIND NONE. HELP ME TURN MY OWN PAIN INTO SOMETHING VALUABLE TO OTHERS. GIVE ME THE PERSPECTIVE AND WISDOM TO SHOW HEALING COMPASSION TO PEOPLE WHO NEED IT. IN JESUS' NAME. AMEN.

THE GIVER OF LIFE

God gives us life and takes us away as He sees fit.
—Johnny Cash

What is the price of two sparrows—one copper coin? But not a single
sparrow can fall to the ground without your Father knowing it. And
the very hairs on your head are all numbered. So don't be afraid;
you are more valuable to God than a whole flock of sparrows.
—Matthew 10:29–31 nlt

In a single sentence, Johnny Cash identifies one of the most challenging truths of the Christian faith: God's sovereignty. God has no boss and does not answer to anyone. He is the ultimate authority, no matter what the subject is. He's not obligated to do anything. He doesn't rely on advisers, focus groups, image handlers, or marketing surveys. He's not motivated by popularity or politics. He does what He wants, when He wants. What's more, everything He does is right and perfect simply because He does it.

How we respond to God's sovereignty—His control of and authority over everything—usually depends on what's going on in our lives. His sovereignty is an awesome and amazing thing when our enemies get what's coming to them. Or when the lab tests bring good news. Or when we nail a job interview. After all, if God has the power to do anything, why would He use it to do something as small and personal as to right our wrongs? Or cause a tumor to be benign? Or help our career? The only conclusion is that He loves us beyond measure and is committed to our well-being.

On the other hand, His sovereignty is a devastating thing when the oncologist says it's time to consider hospice care. Or when the student loan bills mount. Or when politics threaten to tear apart a once-close family. After all, if God has the power to do or change anything, why wouldn't He exercise it to keep three young children from losing their mother? Or to help a deserving person get a college education? Or to keep a family together? The only conclusion is that He doesn't care about us, that there are more important things occupying His attention.

Yet Jesus assures us in Matthew 10 that God *does* care for us. In fact, we are extremely valuable to Him. He knows infinitely more about what we need than we do. He knows exactly how to care for us. There is nothing malicious in His sovereignty. And there's nothing capricious about it, either. He doesn't act on whims or mood swings. He acts according to His will.

Ultimately, God's sovereignty is beyond our comprehension. We may form opinions about what's right and fair, but we have to acknowledge that our opinions carry no weight. That can be a hard thing to accept, because we want answers and explanations that may not be forthcoming.

God's sovereignty must never become an obstacle in our relationship with Him. We don't have to understand His will in order to accept it. If the Bible shows us anything, it's that God can be trusted; He has earned every benefit of the doubt. Our faith in Him is well-placed, and so is our loving gratitude.

HEAVENLY FATHER, I PRAISE YOU FOR YOUR SOVEREIGNTY, YOUR WISDOM, AND YOUR POWER. YOU ANSWER TO NO ONE. YOUR WILL IS PERFECT. YET YOU LOVE US ENOUGH TO CARE ABOUT OUR SORROW AND GRIEF, BECAUSE YOU HAVE EXPERIENCED THEM YOURSELF. I MAY NEVER FULLY UNDERSTAND YOUR WAYS, BUT I TRUST IN YOU. HELP ME MAINTAIN MY TRUST WHEN THINGS GET DIFFICULT. IN JESUS' NAME. AMEN.

Was it for sins that I had done
He groaned upon the tree?
Amazing pity! Grace unknown!
And love beyond degree!

—"Alas, and Did My Savior Bleed"
by Isaac Watts

WEARING YOUR CHRISTIANITY ON YOUR SLEEVE

I am not a Christian artist; I am an artist who is a Christian.
—JOHNNY CASH

"Beware of practicing your righteousness before other people in order to be seen by them, for then you will have no reward from your Father who is in heaven."
—MATTHEW 6:1 ESV

For many people, the word *Christian* comes loaded with no small amount of emotional or cultural baggage. The emotional baggage is usually the result of personal experiences with people who identified themselves as Christians but behaved in an un-Christlike way. No one likes a hypocrite, especially people who have been burned by them. So their attitude toward Christians becomes "Fool me once, shame on you; fool me twice, shame on me." They put up walls to keep Christian acquaintances at a distance. They respond with cynicism when they hear people talk about their faith.

The cultural baggage, on the other hand, usually involves stereotypes about what Christians are like, what they are or aren't allowed to do. Those stereotypes can be restricting, especially for Christian artists. Often when Christians try to break free of those stereotypes, the sincerity of their faith is questioned. They're accused of misrepresenting the Lord.

With this baggage in mind, followers of Christ are faced with a choice in how we present ourselves to others. On the one hand, we can lead with our faith, boldly announcing ourselves as Christians from the outset and inviting people to take us or leave us on our own terms. We cue people to put up their walls, cast a cynical eye our way, and make stereotypical assumptions about us. And then, over time—and with God's help—we work to break down those walls, overcome their cynicism, and defy their stereotypes.

On the other hand, we can take a more subtle approach. We can allow our Christian faith to infuse everything we do, from the personal choices we make to the way we treat the people around us. In other words, we give others an opportunity to see what it looks like to be a servant of Christ before they know we're a servant of Christ. We catch would-be cynics with their guard down and cause them to rethink their attitudes toward the Christian faith. In best-case scenarios, we may even stir up spiritual interest in them.

A popular quote, mistakenly attributed to St. Francis of Assisi, hints at the tension between these two approaches: "Preach the gospel at all times. Use words, if necessary." That's not to suggest that words aren't essential to our Christian witness. They are. But the New Testament writer James said, "Who is wise and understanding among you? By his good conduct let him show his works in the meekness of wisdom" (James 3:13 ESV).

And Jesus Himself said, "In the same way, let your light shine before others, so that they may see your good works and give glory to your Father who is in heaven" (Matthew 5:16 ESV). Jesus doesn't tell us to announce that we have a light. He instructs us to let it shine—to follow His example in the way we live—so that other people will notice it.

> **HEAVENLY FATHER, THANK YOU FOR THE OPPORTUNITY TO IDENTIFY MYSELF WITH YOU—NOT JUST DURING MY LIFE ON EARTH, BUT FOREVER. FORGIVE ME FOR THE TIMES WHEN I FALL SHORT OF CHRISTLIKE BEHAVIOR. BLESS MY EFFORTS TO LIVE MY FAITH IN A WAY THAT ALLOWS OTHERS TO SEE JESUS IN ME. IN HIS NAME. AMEN.**

A FATHER'S IMPACT

My father was a man of love. He always loved me to death. He worked hard in the fields, but my father never hit me. Never. I don't ever remember a really cross, unkind word from my father.

—Johnny Cash

Fathers, do not provoke your children to anger, but bring them up in the discipline and instruction of the Lord.

—Ephesians 6:4 NASB

Because God is our heavenly Father, it makes sense that He would place a high priority on the parent-child relationship. He gave His people the Ten Commandments so they could live life to the fullest. At the center of those commandments is this one: "Honor your father and your mother, so that your days may be prolonged on the land which the Lord your God gives you" (Exodus 20:12 NASB).

Centuries later, the apostle Paul reiterated the importance of the command: "Children, obey your parents in the Lord, for this is right. Honor your father and mother (which is the first commandment with a promise), so that it may turn out well for you, and that you may live long on the earth" (Ephesians 6:1–3 NASB).

However, in the very next verse in Ephesians (quoted above), Paul made it clear that the responsibility for creating a healthy, functional parent-child dynamic is far from one-sided. Parents have a responsibility to make God-honoring decisions in their lives—to conduct themselves in a way that makes their kids want to honor and obey them.

Honorable parenting begins with setting a good example in our relationship with the Lord, by leading our kids in prayer, by reading God's Word with them, by sharing the nuggets of wisdom we discover in our daily Bible study, and by purposefully making—and talking about—God-honoring decisions every day.

Honorable parenting involves instilling in our kids the value of work and of maintaining a sense of integrity and pride in the jobs we do. It involves showing love and compassion to our kids, even and especially when they go astray. It involves recognizing the vulnerability of the young lives in our care and the awesome responsibility and privilege we've been given to prepare them for and guide them through life.

Honorable parenting requires us to set aside our selfish motives and desires. To exercise control over our tongue and emotions. To make tough, unpopular decisions. To be the "bad guy," as needed—and, as such, the recipient of eye rolls, annoyed grunts, and the occasional silent treatment. To recognize that our kids need us as a parent much more than they need us as a friend.

No one is born with the knowledge of how to be a good parent. Some people have an advantage in that they were raised by good parents. However, that's no guarantee that they themselves will be good parents. Likewise, many truly good parents come from dysfunctional family backgrounds.

Good parenting begins with the desire to be a good parent. From there, we can pray and study Scripture to ground our parenting in God's will. We can read parenting books. We can maintain dialogue with other parents through church and social media. We can anticipate parenting challenges before they arise. In short, we can pour ourselves fully into the most important job we'll ever have.

FATHER, THANK YOU FOR THE PRIVILEGE OF CALLING YOU "FATHER." THANK YOU FOR DEMONSTRATING TO ALL PARENTS WHAT IT MEANS TO TRULY LOVE, DISCIPLINE, AND CARE FOR CHILDREN. BLESS MY RELATIONSHIP WITH THE CHILDREN YOU HAVE PLACED IN MY LIFE. GIVE ME THE WISDOM, PATIENCE, AND STAMINA TO BE THE PARENT THEY NEED—ONE WHO WILL BRING GLORY TO YOU. IN JESUS' NAME. AMEN.

STUDY GUIDE

I read novels, but I also read the Bible. And study it, you know? And the more I learn, the more excited I get.
—JOHNNY CASH

Everything in the Scriptures is God's Word. All of it is useful for teaching and helping people and for correcting them and showing them how to live. The Scriptures train God's servants to do all kinds of good deeds.
—II TIMOTHY 3:16–17 CEV

Johnny Cash draws a very important distinction between reading and studying. We all have our favorite novels, magazines, and blogs—reading material that entertains and informs us. However, most of these books, articles, and blurbs don't merit closer study. They don't often reveal hidden truths or open themselves up to life-transforming interpretations. They don't contain the wisdom of Almighty God. And therein lies the difference between everything ever written and the Bible.

That's not to say the Bible can't be read like a novel. Or a history book. Or a law tome. Or a character study. Or a piece of poetry. It can. The Bible is all those things and more. But if we're not careful, we can get locked into a pattern of just reading it, instead of studying and applying it. Case in point: the read-through-the-Bible-in-a-year challenge. It makes for a worthy New Year's resolution, but not everyone benefits from this type of challenge. When reading the Bible becomes something to check off our to-do list, it doesn't make as strong of an impact on our brains, our hearts, or our consciences.

In his second letter to his protégé, Timothy, the apostle Paul offered a glimpse of what the Bible truly is and how we should approach it. For one thing, it's God's Word. The Holy Spirit inspired human authors to write the words of God. He guided the process as the writers used their own unique voices to communicate the given message. Nothing in Scripture originated from human imagination. Everything came directly from God.

For another thing, it's useful for teaching, helping, correcting, and showing us how to live. Because it teaches, its words are worth committing to memory. In Psalm 119:11, the psalmist said to God, "I have hidden Your word in my heart that I might not sin against You" (NIV). We benefit tremendously when we carry the Bible's lessons with us, when we can recall what God would have us do in given situations.

Paul's acknowledgement that the Bible "helps" emphasizes its practical usefulness. Don't let the fact that it contains the wisdom of the ages convince you that it's a mere spiritual or philosophical guide. Perhaps no one has expressed a better approach to Scripture than the New Testament writer James, who wrote, "But don't just listen to God's word. You must do what it says. Otherwise, you are only fooling yourselves" (James 1:22 NLT).

God's Word corrects us when we diverge from the path that God would have us travel. When we start to rely on our own wisdom. When we can't spot the falseness in a false teaching. God's Word is truth. The more time we spend in it, the better equipped we become to spot counterfeits.

The Bible shows us how to live by offering not just practical advice but also real-world examples of the life choices God rewards and the ones that hurt us. And if we take its lessons to heart, it will guide us in our own real-world decision-making. This is the difference between reading and studying. Reading entertains; studying transforms.

HEAVENLY FATHER, THANK YOU FOR THE GIFT OF YOUR WORD—A SOURCE TO TURN TO WHEN I NEED WISDOM, INSTRUCTION, CORRECTION, ENCOURAGEMENT, AND INSPIRATION. CREATE IN ME A HUNGER FOR YOUR TRUTH. GIVE ME THE UNDERSTANDING AND DISCERNMENT TO APPLY IT CORRECTLY IN MY LIFE. IN JESUS' NAME. AMEN.

NO SPECIAL TREATMENT

God's the final judge for Elvis Presley—and Johnny Cash, too. That's solely in the hands of God.

—JOHNNY CASH

But as for you, why do you judge your brother or sister? Or you as well, why do you regard your brother or sister with contempt? For we will all appear before the judgment seat of God. For it is written: "As I live, says the LORD, to Me every knee will bow, and every tongue will give praise to God." So then each one of us will give an account of himself to God.

—ROMANS 14:10–12 NASB

Johnny Cash understood that God is the great Equalizer. The two people he mentioned—himself and Elvis Presley—were larger than life. Or so we're led to believe. He and Elvis were considered icons. Superstars. Incendiary talents who blazed their own trails through this world and left legacies for future generations to enjoy.

Yet one day each man will stand before the Lord, not as an icon or a superstar, but as a created being who will have to answer to his Creator for the things he did and didn't do in his lifetime. While his fame may have singled him out for special treatment on earth, it will carry no weight at the foot of the Lord's throne. Like everyone else who ever lived, each man will face the Lord's judgment.

The first takeaway from this truth is that the urge to put people on pedestals—to view them as being more important or noteworthy than others—is nonsense. No one will be shown special treatment when it really matters. Ultimately, we're all powerless in the face of the Lord's judgment.

The second takeaway is to leave judgment in the hands of the only One qualified to mete it out. Jesus echoes this sentiment in Matthew 7:1–2: "Do not judge, or you too will be judged. For in the same way you judge others, you will be judged, and with the measure you use, it will be measured to you" (NIV).

When we try to usurp God's role as judge, we call down more stringent judgment on ourselves. Our judgment is tainted by our emotions, circumstances, moods, and egos. In many cases, our rush to judge others is an attempt to divert attention away from our own guilt.

The third takeaway is that the prospect of future judgment should impact our present reality. Knowing that one day we will have to answer for the things we do should keep us from making serious mistakes in the here and now. The prospect of judgment also reminds us who sits on the throne of our lives. As Johnny Cash points out, that was important for Elvis Presley to remember. Ultimately, he was not the King; Jesus Christ is. It was also important for Johnny Cash himself to remember. One day the Man in Black would answer to the Lord.

It's essential for us to remember as well. We don't have to be celebrities to be tempted to grab the reins of our lives. Or to think more highly of ourselves than we should. All we need is the wrong mindset at the wrong time. Knowing that one day we will answer for everything we do gives us the perspective we need to make our way through this world in a God-honoring way.

> **HEAVENLY FATHER, ONLY YOU HAVE THE POWER, WISDOM, AND AUTHORITY TO PASS JUDGMENT. YOUR JUDGMENT IS PERFECT; I KNOW THAT. PLEASE HELP ME LIVE WITH A VIEW OF YOUR JUDGMENT ALWAYS BEFORE ME. GUIDE ME IN THE PATHS THAT I SHOULD GO. IN JESUS' NAME. AMEN.**

HERE TO DO GOD'S WILL

*Life is the question, and life is the answer, and
God is the reason, and love is the way.*
—Johnny Cash

*Do not be conformed to this world, but be transformed by the
renewal of your mind, that by testing you may discern what is
the will of God, what is good and acceptable and perfect.*
—Romans 12:2 esv

H is words may sound like a riddle, but Johnny Cash drives home an important point. Too often, we try to complicate simple matters such as the purpose of life, our relationship with God, and our responsibility to others. We mix up our priorities. We look for loopholes in Scripture. We latch on to plausible-sounding excuses. We allow ourselves to be distracted by the trivial pursuits of social media. And in the process, we lose something vital: our sense of direction.

The solution, as is the case with all things spiritual, is to look to the example of Christ. Jesus understood His purpose from the time He was a boy. When He was twelve years old, His family traveled to Jerusalem for the Passover Festival. Afterward, Jesus stayed behind when His parents started their journey home. Joseph and Mary returned to Jerusalem, where they found Jesus in the temple, listening to teachers and asking questions. When His parents told Him that they had been searching for Him, He replied, "Why did you seek Me? Did you not know that I must be about My Father's business?" (Luke 2:49 nkjv).

As an adult, Jesus summarized His earthly ministry this way: "For I have come down from heaven, not to do My own will, but the will of Him who sent Me" (John 6:38 nkjv). Accomplishing God's will was Jesus' top priority, the passion that drove Him.

It should be ours too.

That's what we're created for. That's what life is all about. God designed us so that we would experience genuine, soul-deep fulfillment when we follow the path He's laid out for us and do the work He's equipped us for.

When we feel spiritually lost or aimless, or when we question our purpose in life, the best way to find our footing again is to reconnect with God through prayer and Bible study. That connection is key, because we can do nothing apart from Him. He is our power source. His Holy Spirit equips us with spiritual gifts—specific skills or abilities that we can use to minister. Our responsibility is to nurture those gifts and use them as we serve God and make a difference in the lives of others in His name.

As Johnny Cash points out, love is the way we make others aware of our relationship with God. It's the way we make others aware of His will. The kind of love God calls us to show is sacrificial. It costs us something, whether it be time, energy, or something else. It takes us out of our comfort zones. It compels us to forgive when we would prefer to hold a grudge. To reach out when we would prefer to keep to ourselves. To risk rejection when we'd rather play it safe.

When we pursue God's will, we can look forward to an unpredictable, sometimes scary, sometimes satisfying, sometimes frustrating, but ultimately fulfilling, experience.

> **HEAVENLY FATHER, THANK YOU FOR CREATING ME WITH A PURPOSE. THANK YOU FOR ALLOWING ME TO BE A PART OF YOUR WILL. HELP ME MAINTAIN MY FOCUS ON WHAT YOU WOULD HAVE ME DO SO THAT I CAN MAKE A DIFFERENCE FOR YOUR KINGDOM. IN JESUS' NAME. AMEN.**

THE STRUGGLE

There is a spiritual side to me that goes
real deep, but I confess right up front that
I'm the worst sinner of them all.

—Johnny Cash

The Spirit and your desires are enemies of each other.
They are always fighting each other and keeping
you from doing what you feel you should.

—Galatians 5:17 CEV

In the 1955 film *The Night of the Hunter*, a murderous preacher named Harry Powell, played by Robert Mitchum, has the word *LOVE* tattooed on the knuckles of one hand and the word *HATE* tattooed on the knuckles of the other hand. He explains that the tattoos serve as reminders of the two sides of his nature that are constantly at war.

The apostle Paul confessed to the same struggle, albeit in less dramatic fashion. In addition to the passage from Galatians quoted above, he wrote this:

"I don't understand why I act the way I do. I don't do what I know is right. I do the things I hate. Although I don't do what I know is right, I agree that the Law is good. So I am not the one doing these evil things. The sin that lives in me is what does them.

I know that my selfish desires won't let me do anything that is good. Even when I want to do right, I cannot. Instead of doing what I know is right, I do wrong. And so, if I don't do what I know is right, I am no longer the one doing these evil things. The sin that lives in me is what does them" (Romans 7:15–20 CEV).

Johnny Cash not only experienced this struggle himself, but he made memorable art from it. In songs like "I Walk the Line" and "Folsom Prison Blues," he hints at the tension between doing what's right and giving in to baser instincts that everyone experiences.

Of course, everyone experiences that tension, that struggle, in different ways. For some, it's a fight against addiction, something Johnny Cash knew all too well. For others, it's a habit or temptation that seems to be under control for a while, only to roar back with a vengeance when our defenses are down. For others, it's curiosity or boredom that initiates the struggle.

The Bible assures us that we have the upper hand in these struggles for one simple reason: "Anyone who belongs to Christ is a new person. The past is forgotten, and everything is new" (II Corinthians 5:17 CEV). When we give our lives to Christ, He gives us back something new. Our purposes, feelings, and desires are fresh and different. We see the world in a new way. The things we once loved, we now despise. The sin we once held on to, we now desire to put away forever. That doesn't mean the old person will go down without a fight. What it means is that we have everything we need for victory.

Yet in this struggle lies opportunity. Our changed lives are perhaps our greatest testimony. People who know us recognize that the changes in our lives could only have been made by God. When they see what He's done in our lives, it piques their curiosity and makes them wonder what He could do with the parts of their lives they don't like.

HEAVENLY FATHER, THANK YOU FOR MAKING ME A NEW CREATION IN CHRIST. THANK YOU FOR EQUIPPING ME IN MY STRUGGLE AGAINST MY OLD NATURE. GIVE ME THE STRENGTH AND ENDURANCE TO SUCCEED. HELP ME REMEMBER THE OPPORTUNITY I HAVE TO POINT OTHERS TO YOU THROUGH MY CHANGED LIFE. IN JESUS' NAME. AMEN.

A CHANGE HAS COME

The Master of Life's been good to me. He has given me strength to face past illnesses, and victory in the face of defeat. He has given me life and joy where others saw oblivion. He has given new purpose to live for, new services to render, and old wounds to heal. Life and love go on, let the music play.
—JOHNNY CASH

Dear friends, since God so loved us, we also ought to love one another.
—I JOHN 4:11 NIV

If you had to list the number of ways the Master of Life, as Johnny Cash memorably refers to the Lord, has been good to you, how long would it take you? How long would your list be?

Think of the strength He's given you to overcome illness, injury, and personal struggles. Think of the times He's helped you snatch victory from the jaws of defeat, to succeed when everyone around you was convinced that failure was your destiny. Think of how He shined a light in the darkest of circumstances.

And then ask yourself this: How did He do it? Did He work through miraculous, invisible intervention? Or did He work through other people? Did He equip someone close to you to say or do just the right thing at just the right time? Did He bring a stranger into your life for an unmistakable purpose?

As the preceding words of the apostle John suggest, God intervenes in our lives for reasons beyond merely demonstrating His power and goodness or merely bringing us healing and happiness. He does it to set off a chain reaction. He does with it an eye toward our helping others in turn.

As Johnny Cash points out, the new lease on life that God gives has exciting implications for us—but implications that require work. We have a new purpose to live for. The work that God accomplishes in our lives sets the direction for our new ministry. If He helps us recover from a loss or helps us work through grief, He's positioning us to do the same for others. If He sets us up to be able to speak from experience and truly empathize with hurting people, He wants us to do just that. If He helps us discover our spiritual gifts, He will open the door for us to use them in ways that benefit others.

And if He brings people into our orbits, He wants us to learn to live in peace with them, even if it means healing old wounds. In Matthew 5:23–24, Jesus says, "So if you are about to offer your gift to God at the altar and there you remember that your brother has something against you, leave your gift there in front of the altar, go at once and make peace with your brother, and then come back and offer your gift to God" (GNT). We can't properly worship God until we're properly reconciled with the people in our lives.

Johnny Cash well understood that the key to our fulfillment and joy is to realize that everything God does for us prepares us to do things for others. If we keep His blessings to ourselves, we miss the point—and break God's chain of love.

> **HEAVENLY FATHER, THANK YOU FOR YOUR GOODNESS TO ME. THANK YOU FOR HEALING ME AND TRANSFORMING MY LIFE IN AMAZING WAYS, BOTH BIG AND SMALL. LET ME NEVER LOSE SIGHT OF WHAT YOU HAVE DONE FOR ME. SHOW ME HOW TO FULFILL YOUR PURPOSES FOR ME, HOW TO RENDER NEW SERVICES, AND HOW TO HEAL OLD WOUNDS. IN JESUS' NAME. AMEN.**

LEARNING FROM OUR MISTAKES

I learn from my mistakes. It's a very painful way to learn,
but without pain, the old saying is, there's no gain.
—JOHNNY CASH

Even if good people fall seven times, they will get back up. But
when trouble strikes the wicked, that's the end of them.
—PROVERBS 24:16 CEV

You know who would have nodded in sad agreement with Johnny Cash's admission? David. The beloved second king of Israel. The psalmist and shepherd who killed a fearsome warrior with nothing but a sling and a rock. The ancestor of Jesus. The person God referred to as "a man after My own heart" (Acts 13:22 NIV).

Though David was famous for his heroic loyalty, humility, honor, and devotion to God, he was also guilty of one of the most heinous acts of betrayal in all of Scripture. While a soldier named Uriah in David's army was off fighting a war for his king and his people, David slept with Uriah's wife, whose name was Bathsheba. When Bathsheba became pregnant, David worried that his adultery would be discovered.

David arranged to have Uriah killed in battle so that he could marry Bathsheba—so that people wouldn't question her pregnancy. In his desperation, David lost sight of the fact that nothing can be hidden from God's sight. So David fell, spiritually speaking. And when he fell, he fell hard. The baby he conceived with Bathsheba died.

The consequences of his sin—the death of his son—pushed David to the limits of his endurance. Yet he recognized those consequences as God's discipline and humbly accepted them as such.

That's why he was able to write, "I acknowledged my sin to You and did not cover up my iniquity. I said, 'I will confess my transgressions to the LORD.' And You forgave the guilt of my sin" (Psalm 32:5 NIV). He also wrote, "Create in me a pure heart, O God, and renew a steadfast spirit within me. Do not cast me from Your presence or take Your Holy Spirit from me. Restore to me the joy of Your salvation and grant me a willing spirit, to sustain me" (Psalm 51:10–12 NIV).

Johnny Cash learned from his own experience that God is more concerned with making us right with Him than He is with protecting our feelings. That's why He allows us to face the consequences of our actions. Johnny Cash also learned that discipline can ultimately strengthen our relationship with God.

Even when our mistakes don't involve wrongdoing, we can learn from them. As the passage from Proverbs at the beginning of this devotion points out, the key is to get back up every time we stumble. Every time we do, we build a little more strength. A little more endurance. A little more wisdom, as we learn from each stumble. A little more confidence. A little more character.

Every time we get back up after we stumble, we make ourselves more valuable to other people who stumble. More empathetic. More caring. More watchful.

As Johnny Cash pointed out, we're not defined by our mistakes—but we can be improved by them.

> **HEAVENLY FATHER, THANK YOU FOR NOT GIVING UP ON ME WHEN I STUMBLE. THANK YOU FOR GIVING ME THE OPPORTUNITY TO LEARN AND GROW FROM MY MISTAKES. FORGIVE ME FOR THE TIMES WHEN I FAIL YOU. RESTORE MY RELATIONSHIP WITH YOU. MAKE ME AN INSTRUMENT OF HEALING IN THE LIVES OF OTHERS WHO STUMBLE. IN JESUS' NAME. AMEN.**

On a hill far away stood
an old rugged cross,
The emblem of suffering
and shame;
And I love that old cross
where the dearest and best
For a world of lost sinners
was slain.

—"The Old Rugged Cross"
by George Bennard

POURING IN AND POURING OUT

*Creative people have to be fed from the divine source. I have
to get fed. I had to get filled up in order to pour out.*

—Johnny Cash

*Be still, and know that I am God; I will be exalted among
the nations, I will be exalted in the earth!*

—Psalm 46:10 nkjv

Johnny Cash spoke from the perspective of an artist and a performer. But the point he made applies to everyone. None of us is self-sustaining. None of us possesses a bottomless reservoir of energy, strength, wisdom, motivation, or stamina. For us to function at our highest level, we need to regularly tap into a source who possesses an endless supply of those and other things.

That source, of course, is God Himself. And as we consider the best way to tap into God's resources, we need to look at the example Jesus set during His earthly ministry.

Jesus prioritized time alone with His Father. He chose again and again to give His first and best moments to talking and listening to God in solitude. The fact that we know this about Jesus is no accident. God means for us to know this detail about His Son's personal spiritual rhythms because He means for us to apply them to our lives. The example of Jesus calls His people into rhythms of retreating from the world and entering into it.

The healthy Christian life is neither completely solitary nor completely social. We must learn to withdraw, like Jesus, into isolation to have private quality time with God (Mark 1:35) and then return to the busyness of daily life and the needs of others. We must learn to set aside a regular time for spiritual rest, in some temporarily sacred place, to feed our souls and enjoy God's presence in the stillness. After we address our own spiritual needs, we are able to operate from a position of strength in helping others address theirs.

The retreating is key to this strategy. Some people might point out that since God is everywhere, we can commune with Him anywhere, at any time. Yet while it's true that God can give all of Himself to us anywhere, the perpetual distractions of our noisy culture make it impossible for us to give all of ourselves to Him. That's why the solitude that Jesus sought is essential to us.

Jesus' timing is key too. Read this account of Jesus in Mark 1:35: "Very early the next morning, long before daylight, Jesus got up and left the house. He went out of town to a lonely place, where He prayed" (GNT). The wee hours of the morning gave Jesus the setting He needed for spiritual refreshment and filling. Luke makes it clear that this pattern of retreat and reentry was routine for Jesus: "He would withdraw to desolate places and pray" (Luke 5:16 ESV).

God served as Jesus' source of spiritual nourishment. He fed Jesus so that Jesus could feed others. He poured His wisdom and guidance into Jesus so that Jesus could pour His wisdom and guidance into others. And as Johnny Cash understood, God stands ready to do the same for us. If we want to be a source of spiritual nourishment, support, and encouragement for others, we must turn to God every day for our own nourishment, support, and encouragement.

> **HEAVENLY FATHER, THANK YOU FOR THE INCREDIBLE PRIVILEGE OF SPENDING TIME ALONE WITH YOU. THANK YOU FOR FEEDING ME WHEN I'M SPIRITUALLY UNDERNOURISHED, FOR RECHARGING ME WHEN MY INTERNAL BATTERY RUNS LOW, AND FOR POURING INTO ME SO THAT I MAY POUR INTO OTHERS. GUIDE ME IN YOUR WAYS. IN JESUS' NAME. AMEN.**

THE NATURAL THING TO DO

If you don't get outside every day, even for a minute, you have not appreciated what God has done. It makes you grateful for our surroundings, and it starts your day differently.

—Johnny Cash

I will meditate on Your majestic, glorious splendor and Your wonderful miracles. Your awe-inspiring deeds will be on every tongue; I will proclaim Your greatness.

—Psalm 145:5–6 nlt

Johnny Cash's strong endorsement of nature was more than just a friendly mental health tip. For him, spending time outdoors was more than just a matter of filling his lungs with fresh mountain air or enjoying the warmth of sunshine on his face. Johnny Cash understood that there's something special to be found in nature—something spiritual, something worshipful—that cannot be experienced in human dwellings.

God uses the natural world to reveal aspects of Himself to us. When Job tried to help his friends understand God's character, he pointed to nature. "Just ask the animals, and they will teach you. Ask the birds of the sky, and they will tell you. Speak to the earth, and it will instruct you. Let the fish in the sea speak to you. For they all know that my disaster has come from the hand of the Lord. For the life of every living thing is in His hand, and the breath of every human being" (Job 12:7–10 nlt).

The natural world also gives us a proper perspective of ourselves, as David made so memorably clear in one of his psalms. "When I look at the night sky and see the work of Your fingers—the moon and the stars You set in place—what are mere mortals that You should think about them, human beings that

You should care for them?" (Psalm 8:3–4 NLT). The enormity of God's creation humbles us, but it also underscores His amazing, undeserved, inexplicable love and concern for us.

Our connection with nature runs deep. In fact, it stretches all the way back to creation. Look at Genesis 2:15: "The LORD God put the man in the Garden of Eden to take care of it and to look after it" (CEV). This is more than just a side note in the Genesis narrative. In this verse, we see God's original plan for humanity. He planted a garden of extraordinary beauty and lush vegetation and placed Adam and Eve in it.

But His purpose for them wasn't merely to admire the scenery. God gave them the responsibility to cultivate the garden, to work its soil and nurture its plants. Working in nature was central to God's original plan for humanity.

That plan was ruined one chapter later in Genesis, when Adam and Eve disobeyed God and ate the fruit from the forbidden tree. Sin's curse changed our interaction with nature—and with work. The care and cultivation of the natural world that was once satisfying became a labor-intensive drudgery.

Still, remnants of our original purpose remain. Our connection to nature is part of our DNA. It's hardwired into us. God created us to appreciate and care for the world around us. The first step in fulfilling those purposes is to step outside every chance we get.

> CREATOR OF THE UNIVERSE, I PRAISE YOU FOR YOUR AMAZING WORK. I DELIGHT IN THE BEAUTY AND INTRICACY OF YOUR HANDIWORK. THANK YOU FOR GIVING US UNMISTAKABLE EVIDENCE OF YOUR EXISTENCE AND FOR REVEALING ASPECTS OF YOUR CHARACTER IN YOUR CREATION. DRAW ME CLOSER TO YOU AS I SPEND TIME COMMUNING WITH YOU IN NATURE. IN JESUS' NAME. AMEN.

BE WHAT YOU ARE

You have to be what you are. Whatever you are, you've got to be it.
—Johnny Cash

The human body has many parts, but the many parts make up one whole body. So it is with the body of Christ. Some of us are Jews, some are Gentiles, some are slaves, and some are free. But we have all been baptized into one body by one Spirit, and we all share the same Spirit.
—I Corinthians 12:12–13 NLT

As body parts go, the human big toe is quite unremarkable: two bones, some muscle, a little skin, and a nail. That's pretty much it.

The big toe would certainly seem to pale in comparison to other body parts. It's not nearly as prominent as the eyes. No description of a person ever includes the color or shape of the big toe. It's not nearly as complex as the brain. The big toe performs roughly 10,000 trillion fewer calculations per second. It's not nearly as dramatic as the heart. No one panics when the big toe moves a little faster or a little slower than it normally does. It's not nearly as majestic as the leg. During televised Olympic events, cameras don't zoom in for slow-motion shots of competitors' big toes.

Small, simple, and overlooked, the human big toe might be dismissed as being unimportant, if it weren't for one quirk of our human design. The big toe makes it possible for humans to walk and run upright. It's what separates humans from apes. The big toe plays a critical role in maintaining balance, because it bears most of a person's body weight. The big toe acts as a shock absorber when people walk or run.

If a big toe goes missing or stops working, the entire body suffers. The same principle applies in the church, the body of Christ. As Paul pointed out in

I Corinthians 12:12–13, every believer is part of the body of Christ, regardless of who they are.

Obviously, there's not a one-to-one correlation between the physical human body and the spiritual body of Christ. God doesn't appear to individual believers in dreams to announce, "You're a nostril," "You're a spleen," or "You're a medulla oblongata." The image of Christ's body is intended to show the interconnectedness of His followers and the importance of every person's contributions.

The actual role we play in Christ's body may not be obvious to us. We may not always recognize how we fit together with other parts. But that's not our concern. The Lord makes sure that the various parts of the body work together. Our concern is to do what we do to the best of our ability.

As is the case with the big toe, our work is essential. The rest of the body depends on us. If we don't fulfill our role, the other parts of the body will suffer.

In the big picture, it doesn't matter how other people see you—or even how you see yourself. All that matters is how God sees you. And He sees you as an essential part of the body of Christ. That's why, as Johnny Cash puts it, "you have to be what you are."

HEAVENLY FATHER, THANK YOU FOR CREATING ME WITH A UNIQUE DESIGN AND PURPOSE. THANK YOU FOR GIVING ME A VITAL ROLE IN THE BODY OF CHRIST. GIVE ME THE WISDOM TO UNDERSTAND HOW BEST TO USE MY SKILLS AND ABILITIES WITHIN THE BODY. REMIND ME OF MY IMPORTANCE WHEN I START TO LOSE SIGHT OF IT. IN JESUS' NAME. AMEN.

ONE FOR ALL

We're all in this together if we're in it at all.
—JOHNNY CASH

A friend loves at all times, and a brother is born for a time of adversity.
—PROVERBS 17:17 NIV

"A time of adversity." Those four words, written by Solomon in the book of Proverbs some three thousand years ago, perfectly capture the mood of our culture today. That's why Johnny Cash's quote still resonates.

The systems of this world conspire to pull us apart. Labels are attached to people for convenient division (Republicans and Democrats, conservatives and liberals, Baby Boomers and Millennials, Christians and atheists, Cubs and Cardinals). Lines are drawn. Nonsense is spouted ("If you're not with us, you're against us"). Hearts are hardened.

Social media adrenalizes the process. The immediacy and anonymity of popular social media platforms encourage people to exercise their baser instincts. When they strike a chord, tribes are formed as others respond to them positively or negatively. Elsewhere, chat groups become echo chambers as like-minded people allow their opinions to curdle into dogma that leaves no room for opposing viewpoints.

This splintering of society plays right into the hands of our true enemy. In fact, one of Satan's favorite strategies is to keep people isolated and at odds with each other. That way, he can make us think our struggles are unique, that no one else wrestles with them—or cares about them. If we don't have the right sounding boards in our lives, he can trick us into replaying perceived wrongs, prejudices, and unhealthy attitudes again and again until they take on a life of their own. Given enough time and opportunity, he can get us to hate.

God, on the other hand, works to bring us together. He emphasizes the power of connections. He helps us understand that what unites us is much more powerful than what divides us. We need only to look at His Word to see where He stands.

"Two are better than one, because they have a good reward for their toil. For if they fall, one will lift up his fellow. But woe to him who is alone when he falls and has not another to lift him up! Again, if two lie together, they keep warm, but how can one keep warm alone? And though a man might prevail against one who is alone, two will withstand him—a threefold cord is not quickly broken" (Ecclesiastes 4:9–12 ESV).

That doesn't mean we have to change our core personal beliefs for the sake of feel-good unity. Proverbs 27:17 says, "Iron sharpens iron, and one man sharpens another" (ESV). If we're going to live our lives based on certain assumptions and principles, we need to have them challenged. We need to be able to defend them. We need to be able to understand and respond to people who have equally strong opposing views. But we need to do it in a way that benefits both of us—without rancor or accusations.

We need to "speak the truth in love" (Ephesians 4:15 NLT). That is, we need to be able to communicate God's truth in a way that draws people to us, instead of driving people away. We need to learn to create unity in our diversity.

HEAVENLY FATHER, THANK YOU FOR SURROUNDING ME WITH SO MANY POTENTIAL ALLIES. THANK YOU FOR THE PEOPLE WHO SHARPEN ME AND WHO AREN'T AFRAID TO SPEAK THE TRUTH IN LOVE. GIVE ME THE STRENGTH, WISDOM, AND COURAGE TO DO THE SAME FOR OTHERS. NEVER LET ME FORGET THAT WE'RE ALL IN THIS TOGETHER. IN JESUS' NAME. AMEN.

THE REWARDS OF PERSEVERING

I don't give up because I don't give up. I don't believe in it.
—JOHNNY CASH

So let's not get tired of doing what is good. At just the right time
we will reap a harvest of blessing if we don't give up.
—GALATIANS 6:9 NLT

At first glance, the Bible characters Jonah and Judas Iscariot would seem to have little in common. One was an Old Testament prophet; the other was a New Testament disciple. However, a closer look reveals an unfortunate trait both of them shared. They were inclined to give up.

Jonah received a most distasteful assignment from God: to go to Nineveh, Israel's sworn enemy, and urge the people to repent or face God's judgment. Instead, Jonah booked passage on a ship heading the opposite direction of Nineveh. The last thing he wanted was for Nineveh to repent and be spared God's punishment.

Yet God's will would not be thwarted. Jonah eventually ended up in Nineveh—after spending three days in the digestive system of a giant fish. He preached, the Ninevites repented, and God withheld His judgment—Jonah's worst-case scenario. So Jonah gave up because he didn't get his way. He missed out on the opportunity to celebrate God's amazing grace and forgiveness. Instead, he plopped himself down outside the city and stayed there. His story ends with him sitting under a makeshift shelter, pouting.

Judas Iscariot was chosen by Jesus to be His disciple. He spent three years with the Lord, listening to Him speak, watching Him interact with people, witnessing His miracles. Yet when the opportunity presented itself, Judas committed the most notorious betrayal in human history. For thirty pieces of silver, he turned Jesus over to His enemies. And when Judas realized the gravity of his sin, he gave up—by committing suicide. He missed out on the greatest event in human history—Jesus' resurrection—by a matter of days. Judas's story ends with his lifeless body.

In contrast, we have the story of the Old Testament patriarch Joseph, someone who had every reason to give up. He was sold into slavery by his own brothers. Yet he refused to give up. As a servant in Egypt, he impressed his owner and was put in charge of the household. Just as things were looking up for Joseph, he was falsely accused of sexual assault and thrown into prison. Yet he still refused to give up. He impressed his jailers and his fellow prisoners with his character, his work habits, and his ability to interpret dreams. When the opportunity came to interpret the dreams of Pharaoh, the ruler of Egypt, Joseph was ready.

Joseph's story ends with him saving his family from starvation as the second-in-command over all of Egypt. His forgiving words to his brothers reveal what set Joseph apart from Jonah and Judas Iscariot: "You intended to harm me, but God intended it all for good. He brought me to this position so I could save the lives of many people" (Genesis 50:20 NLT).

Joseph recognized that God can work in and through any situation, no matter how hopeless it seems, to accomplish His will. He can bring about healing, reconciliation, and transformation, even when those things seem unimaginable.

As long as we don't give up. On Him or on ourselves.

HEAVENLY FATHER, THANK YOU FOR NEVER GIVING UP ON ME. GIVE ME THE PERSEVERANCE NEVER TO GIVE UP ON YOU—OR MYSELF. REMIND ME OF YOUR ABILITY TO BRING GOOD FROM ALL CIRCUMSTANCES. IN JESUS' NAME. AMEN.

THE GIFT OF SONG

All music comes from God.
—JOHNNY CASH

I will sing to the LORD as long as I live. I will praise my God to my last breath!
—PSALM 104:33 NLT

Some things can't be expressed by mere speech. Some things affect us so deeply that they call for a different form of communication. They must be put to music. Music offers an outlet for our hopes and dreams, our passions and desires, our struggles and confusion.

Music connects with us on a level nothing else does. It bypasses the filters that keep other things out and stays in our memory long after other things have fallen away. People use music in their search for meaning, artistic expression, pleasure, or relaxation.

The Bible, however, reveals a deeper and more powerful purpose at work when God's people lift their voices in song. For most believers, music plays a central role in glorifying the Lord, offering praise for His great deeds, and creating a sense of unity among worshipers.

The Bible's celebration of music begins in Genesis and continues all the way through to Revelation. What is Adam's exclamation after seeing Eve for the first time? A praise chorus that doubles as a love song (Genesis 2:23). And what are the redeemed in heaven doing as earth's final days come to a close? They sing in worship of the greatness of God (Revelation 15:1–4)?

In between, we find songs for all occasions. When God parted the Red Sea so that the Israelites could cross and then closed it to destroy the Egyptian army, Moses and the people sang out in praise to God, their Deliverer (Exodus 15). When a husband and wife wanted to express their love and desire for one another, they sang the words of the Song of Solomon, along with a female chorus. Jesus Himself sang a song with His disciples (Matthew

26:30).

The best known collection of songs in Scripture is the book of Psalms, which is a compilation of Hebrew poems, lyrics, and prayers. Many psalms were written by David, who, in addition to being a shepherd, giant killer, and king, was also a poet and harpist. When the long-awaited temple was built in Jerusalem, the psalms were used as part of the worship ceremonies (I Chronicles 16:7–36).

Music, as Johnny Cash pointed out, is God's gift to us. And it's the gift that keeps on giving because it draws us closer to Him. The music of worship trains us to recognize and acknowledge who God is and what He's done. The more we sing of His wondrous works, the deeper our appreciation of them grows. Music lends itself to this kind of repetition in ways sermons and prayers cannot.

The beauty of music and song lyrics is that they can pop into our heads any time, seemingly for no reason at all. As a result, we can have impromptu worship sessions several times a day.

Need more convincing?

"I will sing to the LORD as long as I live.

"I will praise my God to my last breath!" (Psalm 104:33 NLT).

"Are any of you suffering hardships? You should pray. Are any of you happy? You should sing praises" (James 5:13 NLT).

"Sing, sing your hearts out to God! Let every detail in your lives—words, actions, whatever—be done in the name of the Master, Jesus, thanking God the Father every step of the way" (Colossians 3:16 THE MESSAGE).

> HEAVENLY FATHER, THANK YOU FOR YOUR GIFT OF MUSIC. THANK YOU FOR CREATING IN ME A SPIRIT THAT IS SOOTHED, INSPIRED, AND COMFORTED BY SONG. I WILL LIFT UP MY VOICE TO YOU IN PRAISE. I WILL SING OF YOUR MAJESTY AND YOUR WORKS. MAY MY SONG BE A JOYFUL NOISE TO YOUR EARS. IN JESUS' NAME. AMEN.

PUT IT IN WRITING
74

*There is nothing in the world more
soul-satisfying than having the kingdom of God
building inside you and growing.*
—Johnny Cash

Let this be recorded for future generations.
—Psalm 102:18 NLT

"Look how much you've grown!" The words every adolescent pretends to be annoyed by but secretly loves to hear. Because growth is important. That's why countless doorframes and walls in homes around the world are permanently marked with lines and dates, recording kids' ever-increasing height.

The funny thing is, the person doing the growing is often the last one to realize it. There is no internal measuring sensor in the brain that suddenly announces, "You just reached 5'7'." So those marks on the wall and those amazed exclamations from people you haven't seen in a while serve a useful purpose. They remind you of how much you've grown.

Spiritual growth—the kind Johnny Cash celebrated—is even harder to recognize. Other people can't always tell what's happening inside you. And you can't measure your soul on a doorframe.

What you can do is keep a written record of your spiritual life, an intimate and honest journal that tracks your highs and lows, your victories and failures, in your walk with Christ.

Journaling can be a key spiritual discipline to support you in your prayer and Bible study. It's also one of the most valuable skills you'll ever develop. Journaling compels you to be an investigative reporter for your own life. To look closely at what happens and ask why. To seek out evidence of God's hand in daily events.

To create a meaningful journal, one that will prove valuable to you in the future, try to work transparency and fearlessness in your writing. Be willing to admit your fears, hopes, doubts, and struggles in an authentic, unselfconscious way. Your goal is to create a snapshot of your spiritual life with each entry. What prayer requests are at the top of your list? What good things are you praising God for? What struggles and distractions are you trying to work through? What worries are taking up space in your brain? What Scripture passages are speaking to you?

Think of your journal as an investment. You add to it a little—or a lot—at a time. A paragraph one day, two full pages another day, depending on the circumstances. Slowly but surely, one volume fills up. And then another. In time, you have a treasure trove of spiritual wealth.

Years from now, perhaps when you're struggling or facing a giant fear in your life, you can look back on your entries. You can be reminded of other struggles that seemed insurmountable at the time. You can reacquaint yourself with big fears that turned out to be rather small. You can see the prayer requests that God answered, in expected and unexpected ways. You can see the ones He didn't answer, much to your relief.

More than anything, though, journaling can give you a sense of how much you've grown in your walk with Christ. The entries in your journal are like marks on the spiritual doorframe of your life.

> **HEAVENLY FATHER, THANK YOU FOR THE FACT THAT THE THINGS YOU'VE DONE IN MY LIFE, THE BLESSINGS YOU'VE SHOWERED ON ME, WOULD FILL VOLUMES. LET ME NEVER FORGET THEM OR TAKE THEM FOR GRANTED. BLESS MY EFFORTS TO KEEP A JOURNAL THAT HONORS YOU. GIVE ME THE WISDOM TO KNOW WHAT TO WRITE—TO KNOW WHAT WILL IMPACT ME WHEN I LOOK BACK ON IT. IN JESUS' NAME. AMEN.**

WHAT IT MEANS TO BE TOUGH

It takes a real man to live for God—a lot more man than to live for the devil, you know? If you really want to live right these days, you've got to be tough.

—JOHNNY CASH

Therefore, since we are surrounded by such a huge crowd of witnesses to the life of faith, let us strip off every weight that slows us down, especially the sin that so easily trips us up. And let us run with endurance the race God has set before us. We do this by keeping our eyes on Jesus, the champion who initiates and perfects our faith. Because of the joy awaiting Him, He endured the cross, disregarding its shame. Now He is seated in the place of honor beside God's throne. Think of all the hostility He endured from sinful people; then you won't become weary and give up.

—HEBREWS 12:1–3 NLT

Johnny Cash raises some provocative questions:

What is a "real man"—or "real woman," as the case may be?
What's the difference between a real man or woman and a wannabe?
What does it mean to "be tough"?
How is that different from counterfeit toughness?

Two thousand years ago, someone answered those questions definitively. He showed the world exactly what a real man is like—and what it means to be tough. And it looked nothing like we would have imagined. The author of Hebrews instructs us to look to Him, so let's look to Him.

Jesus showed us that a tough person takes a radical approach to revenge: "You have heard the law that says the punishment must match the injury: 'An eye for an eye, and a tooth for a tooth.' But I say, do not resist an evil person! If someone slaps you on the right cheek, offer the other cheek also" (Matthew 5:38–39 NLT). A truly tough person resists the urge to hit back—literally or figuratively—even when he has every right to. He absorbs the attacks of others and still makes himself vulnerable to them.

Jesus was tortured before He was crucified. According to Luke 22:63–65, the guards in charge of Jesus beat Him severely. They blindfolded Him and took turns striking Him. After each blow, they demanded that He prove His prophetic skills and identify the man who hit Him. They didn't realize that they were dealing with someone who could have called down a legion of angels to exact revenge on His enemies (Matthew 26:53). Yet Jesus said nothing. He simply absorbed their blows and left revenge to His heavenly Father.

Jesus showed us that a tough person gets rid of his enemies in ways most people wouldn't dream of. He said, "You have heard the law that says, 'Love your neighbor' and hate your enemy. But I say, love your enemies! Pray for those who persecute you!" (Matthew 5:43–44 NLT). This is next-level wisdom. You get rid of your enemies by making them your friends. You reduce the number of opponents in your life by making them allies.

You do that by showing them love when they show you hate. You do it by praying for them before, during, and after your encounters with them. You place their well-being—and your own desire for vengeance—in God's hands. You trust Him to deal with them as He sees fit.

> FATHER, THANK YOU FOR SHOWING US WHAT IT MEANS TO BE TOUGH. GIVE ME THE PATIENCE, UNDERSTANDING, AND PERSPECTIVE TO FOLLOW JESUS' EXAMPLE. HELP ME UNDERSTAND WHAT IT MEANS TO BE TOUGH IN YOUR EYES IN EVERY SITUATION I FACE. IN JESUS' NAME. AMEN.

WHAT DO YOU HAVE TO OFFER?

When you sing, you pray twice.
—Johnny Cash

*So, whether you eat or drink, or
whatever you do, do all to the glory of God.*
—I Corinthians 10:31 esv

Aside from salvation, what's the greatest gift you've ever received? It's a fun question to think about because it allows you to relive some of your favorite birthdays and Christmases. Maybe you found a skateboard under the tree one year. Maybe you got a car for your sweet sixteenth.

If you're feeling romantic, you might nominate your spouse as your best present. If you're a parent, you might put your kids at the top of the list.

All those things would certainly qualify as amazing blessings. However, none of them rise to the rank of the greatest gift (other than salvation) ever. For that, you need to turn to I Corinthians 12:4–7: "Now there are varieties of gifts, but the same Spirit; and there are varieties of service, but the same Lord; and there are varieties of activities, but it is the same God who empowers them all in everyone. To each is given the manifestation of the Spirit for the common good" (esv).

When you put your faith in Christ, you receive a spiritual gift from the Holy Spirit. That gift unlocks your full potential to worship and serve God. It gives you direction in discovering His will for your life. It connects you to the body of Christ, the church.

Johnny Cash understood that his musical and performing abilities were part of his spiritual gift. Every time he put them to use, it felt like a prayer to him. Using his gift in a way that glorified God was, for him, a profound means of communication with his heavenly Father.

You may not have the same spiritual gift that Johnny Cash had, but you have the one the Holy Spirit intends for you. You also have the opportunity to use it as a prayer, as Johnny Cash did. For example, if the Holy Spirit has given you the gift of leadership, you might use it to organize a mentoring program in your church. And every step of the way, as you use your Spirit-given leadership skills, you can keep God foremost in your thoughts. You can pray before making big decisions to include Him in the process. You can offer all glory to Him. That's how you pray using your spiritual gift of leadership.

You can use similar strategies to turn other spiritual gifts into prayers, including teaching, hospitality, and evangelism.

You don't have to do it alone. Not only does the Holy Spirit give you your spiritual gift, but He also helps you turn it into a prayer. The apostle Paul tells us that "the Spirit helps us in our weakness. For we do not know what to pray for as we ought, but the Spirit himself intercedes for us with groanings too deep for words" (Romans 8:26 ESV). The Holy Spirit translates our efforts to pray into language that's acceptable to God.

With your spiritual gift, you can say to the Lord, "Accept my prayer as incense offered to You, and my upraised hands as an evening offering" (Psalm 141:2 NLT).

HEAVENLY FATHER, THANK YOU FOR CREATING IN ME SOMETHING TO OFFER YOU AS A PRAYER. GUIDE MY MOTIVATIONS SO THAT I SEEK NO GLORY FOR MYSELF IN MY PRAYER BUT INSTEAD DIRECT ALL HONOR TO YOU. PLEASE ACCEPT MY HUMBLE BUT HEARTFELT EXPRESSION OF LOVE AND WORSHIP. IN JESUS' NAME. AMEN.

Blessed is the one . . .
whose delight is in the
law of the LORD, and
who meditates on His
law day and night.

—PSALM 1:1–2 NIV

THE REST OF THE STORY

No matter how much you've sinned, no matter how much you've stumbled, no matter how much you fall, no matter how far you've got from God, don't give up. You can still be redeemed. As someone said, keep the faith.

—JOHNNY CASH

Since you have heard about Jesus and have learned the truth that comes from Him, throw off your old sinful nature and your former way of life, which is corrupted by lust and deception. Instead, let the Spirit renew your thoughts and attitudes. Put on your new nature, created to be like God—truly righteous and holy.

—EPHESIANS 4:21–24 NLT

Several years ago, the radio newscaster Paul Harvey hosted a short daily program called *The Rest of the Story*. In each program, he would relate a brief anecdote from history, a biographical sketch, or an overlooked news item. And just when you thought you knew where an anecdote was headed, he would throw in a surprise twist at the end. And then he would sign off by saying, "And now you know . . . the *rest* of the story."

There's no evidence that Paul Harvey borrowed his idea from the authors of Scripture, but it wouldn't have been a surprise if he had. If the Bible teaches us anything, it's that we should always stick around for the rest of the story.

Case in point: the man whose reaction to God's call was "Please send someone else." He claimed to be slow of speech and totally wrong for the job God had in mind. He tried to pawn off his brother as a substitute. Oh, and he was fugitive at the time, wanted for killing a man in a fit of rage.

Case in point: the man whose own betrayal of Jesus on the night of His arrest may have been overshadowed by Judas Iscariot's, but was almost as bad.

He promised to stay by Jesus' side, no matter how bad things got. A few hours later, he went into hiding, leaving Jesus to face His trial and execution alone. This man's checkered past included being called "Satan" by Jesus Himself.

Case in point: the man whose extreme dedication to the Jewish religion drove him to stamp out Christianity before it gained a foothold. He watched and approved of the execution of Stephen, the first Christian martyr. He led a brutally effective campaign to arrest Christian leaders. His name became synonymous with persecution, and he was greatly feared in Christian circles.

What could God possibly do with three people who sinned so egregiously or failed so miserably? Let's see. He used the first man to lead the Israelites out of slavery in Egypt and across the wilderness to the Promised Land. And in so doing, He made the man one of the most revered figures in Jewish history. God used the second man as the cornerstone of the Christian church in the New Testament. He used the third man to plant new churches throughout the Roman Empire (and beyond) in his work as the most influential Christian evangelist ever.

Moses, Peter, and Paul would all heartily agree with Johnny Cash's encouragement to not give up. God will bless your sincere second efforts. And that's the rest of the story.

> **HEAVENLY FATHER, THANK YOU FOR YOUR REDEEMING WORK—FOR NEVER SEEING ANYONE AS A LOST CAUSE. THANK YOU FOR THE EXAMPLES IN YOUR WORD OF PEOPLE WHO REFUSED TO BE DEFINED BY THEIR FAILURES. GIVE ME THE COURAGE AND STRENGTH TO RISE AGAIN EVERY TIME I STUMBLE. MAKE SOMETHING SPECIAL, SOMETHING THAT BRINGS HONOR AND GLORY TO YOU, WITH THE REST OF MY STORY. IN JESUS' NAME. AMEN.**

GENERATIONAL WEALTH

Those who have lived longer than us always have something to teach us, something that we can take with us for the rest of our lives.

—Johnny Cash

"Stand up in the presence of the elderly, and show respect for the aged. Fear your God. I am the Lord."

—Leviticus 19:32 NLT

Of all the natural resources in our world, one that often goes untapped is senior citizens. Johnny Cash recognized what many people don't—that the people of previous generations have much to offer us, if we'll only take the time and effort to discover it.

There is no single, definitive command in Scripture on how to treat older people, but there are quite a few key passages whose truths shed light on the subject. The first is this: "Honor your father and mother. Then you will live a long, full life in the land the Lord your God is giving you" (Exodus 20:12 NLT). To "honor" means to prize someone highly, to care for someone, to show respect to someone, to obey someone.

In Paul's instructions to his protégé, Timothy, he emphasized that this principle of honoring can also be applied to people other than our biological parents. "Never speak harshly to an older man, but appeal to him respectfully as you would to your own father. Talk to younger men as you would to your own brothers. Treat older women as you would your mother, and treat younger women with all purity as you would your own sisters" (I Timothy 5:1–2 NLT).

The second key passage is this: "And now, in my old age, don't set me aside. Don't abandon me when my strength is failing" (Psalm 71:9 NLT). Let's face it. We live in a young person's world. But we can't allow older generations to be cast aside for the simple crime of getting older. We have a responsibility to be there for them the way they were there for us.

The third key passage is this: "Tune your ears to wisdom, and concentrate on understanding. Cry out for insight, and ask for understanding. Search for them as you would for silver; seek them like hidden treasures" (Proverbs 2:2–4 NLT). Previous generations are gold mines of wisdom, hard-earned from life experiences that we may never have. We can learn from their triumphs, their losses, and their mistakes. We can discover from talking with them that there's nothing new under the sun. Human nature, and the struggles that go with it, aren't much different today than they were fifty years ago. Or two hundred years ago. Only the details and context change. Greed is greed. Prejudice is prejudice. Temptation is temptation. If we humble ourselves and acknowledge that the experiences of older people can be signposts for our own lives, we will uncover a wealth of applicable wisdom.

The fourth key passage is this: "And the King will say, 'I tell you the truth, when you did it to one of the least of these My brothers and sisters, you were doing it to Me!'" (Matthew 25:40 NLT). We need to recognize the ministry opportunities we have with older people. Those opportunities begin with acknowledging their contributions and making sure they feel seen, respected, and cared for.

> **HEAVENLY FATHER, THANK YOU FOR THE WISDOM AND GUIDANCE I'VE RECEIVED FROM MY ELDERS. THANK YOU FOR THE CARE FOR THEM YOU SHOW IN YOUR WORD. HELP ME STAY HUMBLE IN SPIRIT SO THAT I CAN LEARN FROM THEM. GIVE ME THE WISDOM AND DISCERNMENT TO KNOW HOW I CAN SERVE THEM. IN JESUS' NAME. AMEN.**

HOME-FIELD ADVANTAGE

*The battle against the dark one and the clinging to
the right One is what my life is about.*
—JOHNNY CASH

*This is the message which we have heard from Him and declare
to you, that God is light and in Him is no darkness at all. If we
say that we have fellowship with Him, and walk in darkness,
we lie and do not practice the truth. But if we walk in the light
as He is in the light, we have fellowship with one another,
and the blood of Jesus Christ His Son cleanses us from all sin.*
—I JOHN 1:5–7 NKJV

One of the cornerstone principles of sporting competitions is home-field advantage—the tendency of players and teams to enjoy more success in their own facilities than they do in other people's facilities. Though the theories for why competitors enjoy a home-field advantage vary, the results are hard to argue with. In some cases, the winning percentage for teams at home is as high as 70 percent. It seems that familiarity and comfort in a given setting have a direct correlation to victory.

That goes for spiritual battles as well as sporting ones. In his stark admission, Johnny Cash hints at the home-field advantage Satan exploits in his spiritual warfare against God's people. He is the "dark one," because he prefers to work in the shadows. Darkness is his ally.

His preferred battle strategy is to pull us into darkness with him. So he tempts us with habits that cause us to feel shame, things we prefer to keep hidden. He encourages us to sneak around and live double lives—upstanding on the outside, but vulnerable to our lusts and desires on the inside. The more secrets we have to keep, the more drawn to darkness we'll be. And darkness is where Satan does his best work.

Our wisest counterstrategy is to move the battle to God's venue, where we can enjoy home-field advantage. Spiritual battles fought in the light are ours for the taking, as the apostle John made clear in his first letter (I John 1:5–7).

Jesus is light. He said so in John 8:12: "I am the light of the world. He who follows Me shall not walk in darkness, but have the light of life" (NKJV). Nothing is hidden from Him. His light reveals everything about us, including the things we'd prefer to keep in the darkness. But the light nudges us toward repairing and strengthening our relationship with Christ.

The light reveals our need to confess our sins and seek God's forgiveness. When we do, "He is faithful and just to forgive us our sins and to cleanse us from all unrighteousness" (I John 1:9 NKJV).

"All unrighteousness"—that's important. With no unrighteousness—no darkness—to work with, Satan loses his home-field advantage. He loses his most effective weapon against us. Satan can't stand the glare of all-encompassing light. He can't stand to have his ways exposed for everyone to see. His only option is to flee, to go back to the shadows and lie in wait, hoping that we will wander away from God's light and into his home field again.

> JESUS, YOU ARE LIGHT, AND I PRAISE YOU FOR THAT. YOU ILLUMINATE THE DARK PLACES IN MY LIFE SO THAT I CAN BRING THEM TO THE LIGHT AND FIND FORGIVENESS AND HEALING. GUIDE ME IN YOUR WAYS SO THAT I REMAIN IN YOUR LIGHT. KEEP ME FROM THE DARK PLACES, WHERE I'M VULNERABLE TO THE ATTACKS OF MY ENEMY. IN YOUR NAME. AMEN.

HANDLING THE TRUTH

Anyone who really wants the truth ends up at Jesus.
—Johnny Cash

Do your best to present yourself to God as one approved, a worker who has no need to be ashamed, rightly handling the word of truth.
—II Timothy 2:15 ESV

The American Film Institute created a list of the one hundred most memorable movie lines of all time. At number 29 is an unforgettable line from the 1992 film *A Few Good Men*. In a tense courtroom scene near the end of the movie, a Navy lawyer, played by Tom Cruise, interrogates an arrogant Marine colonel, played by Jack Nicholson. Enraged by the lawyer's persistent badgering for the truth, the colonel bellows, "You can't handle the truth!"

And a legendary quote was born.

Those five words may resonate especially powerfully with Christians who have faced dark nights of the soul as they came to grips with the gospel message and their walk with Christ. Before anyone can embark on that journey, they have to acknowledge some extremely difficult truths.

First, there's the truth that we're all sinners who deserve punishment for our sin. No one expressed that truth better than the apostle Paul: "For all have sinned and fall short of the glory of God" (Romans 3:23 ESV). "For the wages of sin is death, but the free gift of God is eternal life in Christ Jesus our Lord" (Romans 6:23 ESV). According to God's perfect justice, everyone is guilty of sin, and sin must be punished by death. So the first difficult truth is this: every one of us is born under a death penalty.

Second, there's the truth that our good works can't change our standing before God. People with a can-do attitude like to believe that no situation is hopeless or beyond our ability to fix, if we just work hard enough. The Bible makes it clear that that's not the case. "All of us have become like one who is unclean, and all our righteous acts are like filthy rags; we all shrivel up like a leaf, and like the wind our sins sweep us away" (Isaiah 64:6 NIV). No matter how many good works we perform, we can never be good enough in God's eyes. His standard is absolute perfection, and we can't come close. We are helpless to save ourselves. And that's a hard truth to handle.

Third, there's the truth that Jesus had to die for what we did. The apostle Peter expressed that truth this way: "For Christ also suffered once for sins, the righteous for the unrighteous, to bring you to God. He was put to death in the body but made alive in the Spirit" (I Peter 3:18 NIV). Jesus came to earth and lived a sinless life. In doing so, He became the perfect sacrifice—the only sacrifice God would accept for the sins of the world. So the only innocent person who ever lived paid the price of sin so that anyone who puts their trust in Him can have eternal life with God. That's the most important truth of all.

> **HEAVENLY FATHER, YOU ARE THE SOURCE OF ALL TRUTH. THERE IS NO LIE TO BE FOUND IN YOU OR YOUR WORD. THANK YOU FOR GIVING ME A FOUNDATION OF TRUTH TO BUILD MY LIFE ON. GUIDE ME AS I PROCESS THE TRUTH OF THE GOSPEL AND APPLY IT TO MY LIFE. HELP ME SHARE THAT TRUTH WITH OTHERS. IN JESUS' NAME. AMEN.**

HOW MUCH IS ENOUGH?

*Everything I have and everything I do
is now given completely to Jesus Christ.*
—Johnny Cash

*Each of you should give as you have decided in your heart to give. You
should not be sad when you give, and you should not give because
you feel forced to give. God loves the person who gives happily.*
—II Corinthians 9:7 ncv

Many people balk at the idea of giving back to God. They reckon that God Himself doesn't need anything we have to offer. They point to certain televangelists who seem to be "fleecing the flock." And they keep their guard up when the offering is taken in church. They approach giving in the same way they approach taxes: pay as much as you have to so that you don't get in trouble, but no more. And that amount, as many see it, is the tithe—10 percent of their weekly income. The tithe, in effect, becomes their "dues" for attending church.

The problem with that mindset is that it overlooks a few very important truths. The first is that giving, as Johnny Cash points out, involves more than just money. It involves time, energy, and talents too. All those things have been given to us by God, and all can be used for His service.

The second truth is that everything we own belongs to God. One problem with fixating on the 10 percent figure is that we start to believe that the other 90 percent belongs to us, to do with as we please. The reality is that 100 percent belongs to God. We don't own anything. We're simply managers of what God has given us.

The third truth is that as God's managers, we should seek the highest rate of return with God's resources. Many wealthy people rely on experts to manage their money for them. Managers typically earn a percentage of the assets they invest. If managers do well in their investments, they receive a bigger income. They have a strong incentive to seek good returns for the people they are investing for. The same truth applies to us as God's managers. We should seek the highest rate of return, because we'll earn a higher reward for eternity.

That was the principle behind Jesus' parable of the three servants in Matthew 25. Before the master left for a long journey, he divided his assets among his three servants. The first was given five talents—roughly four hundred pounds of gold. He invested them and doubled what was entrusted to him. The second servant was given two talents. He, too, invested them and doubled the assets entrusted to him. The third servant was given one talent. He buried it, just to be safe. He gave back to his master exactly what had been given to him—and nothing more. The master congratulated the first two servants and condemned the third. He then wisely took the third servant's talent and gave it to the first servant.

Jesus' point was this: one day we'll give an account of what we did with the time, opportunities, and financial resources that God entrusted to us. So we should seek the highest rate of return from those things, in terms of accomplishing God's work and furthering His kingdom.

Ultimately, the question is not "How little can I give back to God?" but rather "How much can I give and invest in God's kingdom?"

> **FATHER, THANK YOU FOR ENTRUSTING ME WITH YOUR RESOURCES. BLESS MY EFFORTS TO SEEK THE HIGHEST RATE OF RETURN FOR YOU. GIVE ME THE WISDOM TO KNOW WHAT TO DO WITH WHAT YOU'VE GIVEN ME. IN JESUS' NAME. AMEN.**

MORE THAN ONE WAY
TO PREACH A SERMON

In my world of religion, you're called by God to preach or you don't preach. I've never been ordained by God to preach the gospel. I have a calling; it's called to perform and sing.
—Johnny Cash

Make your light shine, so that others will see the good that you do and will praise your Father in heaven.
—Matthew 5:16 CEV

Once upon a time, preachers were a favorite target of comedians. There were certain clichés about what a preacher looked like or how he talked that were always good for a laugh. Robin Williams built several memorable routines on the foibles of preachers.

Times have changed, though. Styles have changed. In many churches today, you'd be hard-pressed to identify which one was the preacher onstage if you'd never been to the church before.

Yet some stigmas remain. And for many people, the prospect of being a preacher is not only undesirable; it's unimaginable.

Johnny Cash understood that being a preacher—one whose responsibilities include searching Scripture for applicable material to share with a congregation, thinking up new and creative ways to express ancient truths, preparing sermons week after week, delivering messages with a practiced cadence that holds people's attention, and knowing how to "read" a congregation—is a calling. And he recognized that it was a calling he hadn't received.

Beyond his quote, however, lies a truth that all believers must come to grips with: we all preach; we just do it in different ways. We preach with our lives. Or, as Jesus put it in Matthew 5, we preach by letting our light shine so that others can see it and be drawn to God because of it.

Untold number of Christians shine their lights every day. They forgive those who hurt them. They share their resources with people in need. They give without asking for anything in return. They listen to those who are suffering. They pray for the people around them who are struggling in life. And when they are given the opportunity, they give people the reason for their kindness, their patience, their forgiveness, and their love—they point them to Jesus and to the truths in God's Word.

These people preach the gospel with the way they live. They preach it by letting their lights shine.

The long-retired elder who still makes his way, slowly and painfully, to his small church every Sunday, always arriving early to help prepare for worship services and greet his fellow worshipers.

The high schooler who shovels snow and salts sidewalks for his elderly neighbors, but always refuses payment.

The shy sixth grader whose heart for others compels her to sit down next to kids who are sitting by themselves at lunch and strike up conversations and friendships.

The businesswoman who prefers to remain anonymous when she pays for the groceries of a struggling single mother or for the meals of a soldier and his family in a restaurant.

The passerby who doesn't pass by the homeless person holding a sign on the sidewalk but instead stops to talk, to discover the person's story, to find ways to help.

These people, and countless others like them, reveal Christ in ways few sermons ever could. And so do you, when you let your light shine.

HEAVENLY FATHER, THANK YOU FOR THE PEOPLE WHO PREACH TO ME EVERY DAY WITHOUT EVEN REALIZING IT. THANK YOU FOR THE PEOPLE WHO, BY SIMPLY GOING ABOUT THEIR DAILY LIVES, SHOW ME TRUTHS ABOUT WHAT IT MEANS TO BE LOVING AND COMMITTED AND HONORABLE AND GODLY. HELP ME DO THE SAME FOR OTHERS. MAKE ME CONSTANTLY AWARE OF THE OPPORTUNITY I HAVE TO SHARE MY FAITH IN THE WAY I LIVE. IN JESUS' NAME. AMEN.

OURS FOR THE TAKING

The way God has given it to me, life is a platter—a golden platter laid out there for me. It's been beautiful.
—JOHNNY CASH

I can do all things through Christ who strengthens me.
—PHILIPPIANS 4:13 NKJV

A quick online search revealed that, in addition to being a platter, life is also . . . a highway; a rock; an adventure; like a box of chocolates; like a camera; like a mirror; like a piano; like a book; like a garden; like a game of cards; like a jigsaw puzzle; a short, warm moment; quite absurd; and a cabaret, old chum.

Yet Johnny Cash's analysis gets to the heart of an important truth. God has laid out for us an amazing array of things to do, places to go, people to meet, skills to acquire, lessons to learn, and wisdom to gain. It's all ours for the taking.

To make the most of that opportunity, we need to understand just how big God's "golden platter" is. One of the great temptations of life is to reach only for what's right in front of us. Consciously or unconsciously, we sometimes limit our perspective as to how much is actually available to us. Sometimes our vision is obscured by a less-than-privileged upbringing. Sometimes it's blurred by physical or emotional challenges. Sometimes it's blurred by fear or insecurity.

Whatever it is that obscures our perspective, the result is that we assume only a limited amount of God's platter offerings are available to us. That we'll get our hand slapped if we try to reach for more. So we claim the few things we can see and assume that's all God wants us to have.

But that's not what God wants. Look at the invitation He extends in Psalm 34:8: "Oh, taste and see that the LORD is good; blessed is the man who trusts in Him!" (NKJV). Those aren't the words of One who wants to limit our platter gatherings. Those are the words of One who wants us to see how much we can grab!

Don't let the "golden" aspect of Johnny Cash's analogy throw you. This isn't about fame or fortune. The golden platter of life has nothing to do with material possessions. It has to do with contentment, loving relationships, the productive use of our God-given talents, a continuously growing relationship with Christ, and the security that comes from knowing nothing can separate us from our heavenly Father.

"Taste and see that the LORD is good" is an invitation to explore the boundaries of God's goodness—the full dimensions of His golden platter. We do that through His Word. In the pages of Scripture, we find promises like this: "I know what I'm doing. I have it all planned out—plans to take care of you, not abandon you, plans to give you the future you hope for." (Jeremiah 29:11 THE MESSAGE). We find the stories of Esther, the humble Jewish woman who married the king of Persia and saved her people, and David, the young shepherd who became Israel's greatest king.

Esther and David (and many other Bible characters) recognized what God had laid out before them. They dared to taste and see that the Lord is good. And what they discovered changed not only their own lives but the lives of countless others. Let's praise God that the same opportunity is available to us.

> **HEAVENLY FATHER, THANK YOU FOR THE OPPORTUNITIES YOU'VE LAID OUT FOR ME. THANK YOU FOR MAKING SO MANY THINGS POSSIBLE FOR ME. GIVE ME THE SPIRITUAL VISION TO RECOGNIZE WHAT'S AVAILABLE TO ME AND THE COURAGE TO PURSUE IT. IN JESUS' NAME. AMEN.**

CHASING THE WIND

*It's all fleeting. As fame is fleeting, so are all the trappings of
fame fleeting—the money, the clothes, the furniture.*
—Johnny Cash

*Anything I wanted, I would take. I denied myself no pleasure. I even found
great pleasure in hard work, a reward for all my labors. But as I looked at
everything I had worked so hard to accomplish, it was all so meaningless—
like chasing the wind. There was nothing really worthwhile anywhere.*
—Ecclesiastes 2:10–11 NLT

What do boxer Mike Tyson, soccer legend Diego Maradona, golfer John Daly, basketball star Dennis Rodman, and Olympic gold medalist Dorothy Hamill have in common? They all learned the hard way the truth of Johnny Cash's words. Each of these superstars made fortunes in their respective sports—and then lost it all. Every one of them went broke.

Likewise, there are more than a few lottery winners who discovered how fleeting money can be. The West Virginia construction worker who won $314 million and lost it all. The Kentucky man who won $27 million and five years later was penniless and living in a storage shed with his wife. The New Jersey woman who won *two* multimillion-dollar prizes and still managed to blow it all on gambling and bad investments.

Social media stars who have "gone viral" and become famous overnight often discover that the virus passes as quickly as it comes on. They enjoy their proverbial fifteen minutes of fame and then disappear from the public eye.

"Here today, gone tomorrow" is a difficult reality to face. Fortunately for us, God has filled His Word with truths that help us put fame and fortune in perspective. One truth is found in the Ecclesiastes passage quoted above. Few people understood the fleeting pleasures of fame and fortune better than Solomon, who was blessed by God with extraordinary wisdom, wealth, and fame. Solomon chased the pleasures that came from those blessings with everything he had—and came up empty. "Meaningless" is a pretty powerful descriptor. When Solomon turned his extraordinary wisdom inward, he realized that his fame and fortune added nothing substantial, lasting, or worthwhile to his life.

Jesus' warning in Matthew 6:19–20 gives us another truth to consider: "Don't store up treasures here on earth, where moths eat them and rust destroys them, and where thieves break in and steal. Store your treasures in heaven, where moths and rust cannot destroy, and thieves do not break in and steal" (NLT). In other words, if we prioritize material possessions—homes, cars, clothes, vacations, and shiny things—we will regret it. Inevitably, those things will wear out, lose value, get stolen, or be left behind. But if we prioritize the things of God and His work, we will be set for eternity.

A third truth is found in Jesus' parable of the wise and foolish builders. The wise builder built his house, his life, on rock—that is, the solid foundation of God's truth and priorities. And when the storms of life blew, his house stayed standing. The foolish builder built his house, his life, on sand—that is, the unreliable foundation of things like fame and fortune. When the storms of life blow, those things aren't strong enough to support us. Ultimately, they will cause us to collapse.

If we want to build something lasting, we have to use the things of God.

HEAVENLY FATHER, THANK YOU FOR THE ETERNAL TREASURES THAT AWAIT ME. THANK YOU FOR THE WARNINGS IN YOUR WORD ABOUT THE ULTIMATE WORTHLESSNESS OF EARTHLY TREASURES. HELP ME HEED THOSE WARNINGS WHEN I'M TEMPTED TO PURSUE MATERIAL THINGS. GIVE ME YOUR PERSPECTIVE ON WHAT'S TRULY VALUABLE. IN JESUS' NAME. AMEN.

MAKING THE MOST OF DOUBT

I recently found myself going through a period of uncertainty about my future as a performer, my status as a personality, the believability of my Christian witness, and the knowledge of God's will in my life. I felt a force bigger than myself saying, "Lay back. Take it easy. Study hard. Read your Bible. Think, write, and keep your mouth shut for a while."

—JOHNNY CASH

Be merciful to those who doubt.

—JUDE 1:22 NIV

Doubt gets a bad rap. It's not usually mentioned as a quality people admire in others. Calling someone a doubter is rarely intended as a compliment. And that's a shame because, as Johnny Cash discovered, doubt often results in a stronger faith.

We see that in the biblical encounter that landed "doubting Thomas" his nickname. The first time Jesus appeared to His disciples after His resurrection, His disciple Thomas was absent. Later, when the other disciples told him about the encounter, Thomas replied, "I won't believe it unless I see the nail wounds in His hands, put my fingers into them, and place my hand into the wound in His side" (John 20:25 NLT).

The Gospel of John offers few clues as to Thomas's tone. Was it defiant? Did he dig his heels in and refuse to be pushed past the limits of his logic and reason? Was it condescending? Did he see himself as the lone voice of reason in a group that was suffering some kind of mass hysteria? Was it anguish? Did he desperately want to believe their story but couldn't bring himself to do it, for fear of disappointment? Doubt presents itself in many ways and for many reasons.

More important than the tone of Thomas's doubt was the response he received. Eight days later, Jesus appeared to His disciples again. This time, Thomas was there. Jesus didn't angrily confront Thomas or berate him for his weak faith. He didn't kick him out of the room or tear up his disciple membership card.

Instead, Jesus said to Thomas, "Put your finger here, and look at My hands. Put your hand into the wound in My side. Don't be faithless any longer. Believe!" (John 20:27 NLT).

Thomas had no way of knowing it at the time, but he would play a large role in spreading Jesus' message far beyond Jerusalem. According to church tradition, Thomas became a missionary to India, where he was eventually put to death by Hindu priests.

Thomas's later ministry was made possible by Jesus' gracious response to his early doubt. That day in the closed room, with the other disciples looking on, Jesus said, in essence, "Thomas, I have big plans for you. But your doubts are going to get in the way and keep you from reaching your potential. So do whatever you need to do to overcome those doubts. You asked for proof, and here it is. But now that you know the truth, never let it go."

Those words dovetail nicely with the words Johnny Cash received. When doubt rears its head, there's no need to panic or beat yourself up with guilt. Instead, take your questions and concerns to the Source of truth. Read His Word. Spend time in conversation with Him. Ask Him to help you work through your doubts and strengthen your faith.

In other words, do what you need to do so that you're ready to accomplish the big plans Jesus has for you.

HEAVENLY FATHER, THANK YOU FOR BEING UNDERSTANDING WHEN I STRUGGLE WITH DOUBT. THANK YOU FOR THE RESOURCES YOU'VE MADE AVAILABLE TO HELP ME STRENGTHEN MY FAITH. HELP ME WORK THROUGH MY DOUBT AND EMERGE STRONGER SO THAT I CAN HELP OTHERS WHO STRUGGLE. IN JESUS' NAME. AMEN.

Lead me gently home, Father,
Lead me gently home,
When life's toils are ended,
And parting days have come,
Sin no more shall tempt me,
Ne'er from Thee I'll roam,
If Thou'lt only lead me, Father,
Lead me gently home.

—"Lead Me Gently Home",
by Will L. Thompson

PARENTAL GUIDANCE

I knew I wanted to sing when I was a very small boy—when I was probably four years old. My mother played a guitar, and I would sit with her, and she would sing, and I learned to sing along with her.

—Johnny Cash

Listen, my son, to your father's instruction and do not forsake your mother's teaching. They are a garland to grace your head and a chain to adorn your neck.

—Proverbs 1:8–9 NIV

Some traits and characteristics that we inherit from our parents are obvious—red hair, prominent jaw, small earlobes. Some are less obvious—a preference for country living, a fondness for extra spicy food, an introverted personality. Or, in the case of Johnny Cash and his mother, a love of music. As parents, we need to recognize that these less obvious inherited traits and characteristics are every bit as central to our children's identity as the obvious ones are. For better or worse.

"Start children off on the way they should go, and even when they are old they will not turn from it" (Proverbs 22:6 NIV). Parents have an overwhelming advantage over almost any other would-be influence in our kids' lives. We have virtually unlimited access to them during their formative years. We have the opportunity to mold them when they're most malleable. We are the go-to sources for answers when they first start to ask the important questions of life.

God has entrusted us with a sacred duty and a vital assignment. If we aren't awed and humbled by the responsibilities of parenthood—and perhaps a little leery of the power that comes with it—we may not fully grasp its importance.

Guiding our children "on the way they should go" begins with recognizing that they have been uniquely gifted by God. To do that, we must set aside our own frustrated hopes and dreams. We must resist the temptation to see our children as an extension of ourselves or to take a one-size-fits-all approach to parenting more than one child.

Every child deserves our best. Our sons and daughters need us to see them for the people they are, not for who we want them to be. That takes a tremendous amount of time and effort. But that's why parents get paid the big bucks.

The best way to make that happen is expose your children to a variety of opportunities, in a variety of settings. You do that by sharing your love of various things—as Johnny Cash's mother did with music—often enough so they can discover their own passions and abilities. Plant the seeds of interest and see which ones grow. And then encourage other trusted loved ones to do the same.

As your children start to discover their gifts, abilities, and interests, you can continue to support them in the way they should go by providing encouragement along the way. By becoming a reliable jet stream of positivity to help them power past the headwinds of doubt and discouragement they encounter along the way.

Starting your "children off on the way they should go" means keeping them grounded in God's Word and conscious of His blessings. It involves leading your children to thank God continuously for the gifts they've been given.

HEAVENLY FATHER, THANK YOU FOR THE OPPORTUNITY YOU GIVE PARENTS TO MAKE A HUGE IMPACT ON THE LIVES OF THEIR CHILDREN. THANK YOU FOR THE WORDS OF WISDOM IN SCRIPTURE THAT GIVE DIRECTION TO PARENTS. GUIDE ME IN MY PARENTAL DECISION-MAKING. HELP ME UNLOCK MY CHILDREN'S POTENTIAL AND DISCOVER THE GIFTS YOU'VE GIVEN THEM. IN JESUS' NAME. AMEN.

THE PURSUIT OF INDEPENDENCE

You've got to know your limitations. I don't know what your limitations are. I found out what mine were when I was twelve. I found out that there weren't too many limitations, if I did it my way.

—JOHNNY CASH

Jesus replied, "I tell you the truth, everyone who sins is a slave of sin. A slave is not a permanent member of the family, but a son is part of the family forever. So if the Son sets you free, you are truly free."

—JOHN 8:34–36 NLT

The *Twilight Zone* is one of the best-loved shows from the Golden Age of television. In many markets, you can still watch episodes every night. That's pretty impressive longevity for a show that debuted in the 1950s. One of the reasons for its continuing popularity is the plot twists the writers liked to throw in at the end of episodes.

"A Nice Place to Visit" is a case in point. The episode tells the story of Rocky Valentine, a sociopathic menace who's killed robbing a pawn shop. He wakes up in the afterlife to find he has a "guardian angel," as Rocky calls him, who introduces Rocky to his new private paradise. In this place, everything goes Rocky's way. Every time he gambles, he wins. Any woman he wants is available to him. And when he starts committing crimes, he always gets away with them because his victims play along. The sheer predictability of his situation soon drives Rocky mad. Everything is too perfect. In desperation, he pleads with his guardian angel, pointing out that he deserves to be in "the other place"—that is, hell. The angel laughs demonically and informs him that he *is* in the other place.

This notion of an unexpected twist plays into the topics of Johnny Cash's quote: freedom and independence. Many people believe that they know what freedom looks and feels like, so they pursue it as their God-given right. Operating under the assumption that they have the wisdom, perspective, and foresight to determine what's best for them, they take steps to become independent.

The twist is that what seems like freedom to them is actually slavery to sin, as Jesus explains in John 8. Their sinful nature blinds them to the truth and convinces them that they know at least as much as God does about what's best for them.

The mistake they make is confusing freedom for autonomy. God has given us plenty of freedom, but that doesn't mean we're in control of our lives. Or should be. People chase autonomy in different ways, including pursuing financial independence, trying to master their health, and figuring out how they can be left alone to do their own thing.

The problem is, God calls us to a life of radical *dependence*. He wants us to run to Him, to need His guidance and mercy. That's why the writer of Hebrews offers this encouragement: "So let us come boldly to the throne of our gracious God. There we will receive His mercy, and we will find grace to help us when we need it most" (Hebrews 4:16 NLT).

God encourages us to enjoy the freedom He's given us. But He has no reason to support our independence movement. He has no desire to be unnecessary in our lives.

> **HEAVENLY FATHER, THANK YOU FOR THE FREEDOM YOU GIVE ME. MORE THAN THAT, THANK YOU FOR NOT GIVING ME INDEPENDENCE. REMIND ME OF THE PRIVILEGE I HAVE OF APPROACHING YOUR THRONE BOLDLY TO ASK FOR YOUR HELP. OPEN MY EYES WHEN I START TO CONFUSE SLAVERY TO SIN FOR FREEDOM. KEEP ME ALWAYS DEPENDENT ON YOU. IN JESUS' NAME. AMEN.**

A PLACE JUST FOR YOU AND GOD

I love to go to the studio and stay there ten or twelve hours
a day. I love it. What is it? I don't know. It's life.
—Johnny Cash

"Here's what I want you to do: Find a quiet, secluded place so
you won't be tempted to role-play before God. Just be there as
simply and honestly as you can manage. The focus will shift
from you to God, and you will begin to sense His grace."
—Matthew 6:6 The Message

Johnny Cash had the recording studio. What's your special place? Where could you spend ten hours at a time, given the opportunity? Where do you experience life in a more meaningful way?

If this were a *Family Feud* question, answers might include "Beach," "Garden," "Cozy reading nook," and maybe even "Moving vehicle," if one of the contestants was a long-haul trucker. The point is, we all have places where we feel most comfortable. Jesus' suggestion in Matthew 6 is to invite God to join us there.

Jesus leaves most of the details to us. The one specific instruction He gives is to find a quiet, secluded place—not for God's sake, but for ours. The best way to approach God is with an attitude of complete openness, honesty, and vulnerability. The presence of other people can interfere with that approach.

What happens, if we're not careful, is that we start to become aware of our surroundings and the people in them. And our desire to look busy communicating with God and meditating on His Word for their benefit can supersede our actual communication and meditation.

Seclusion also frees us from distractions. That's why it's ideal to choose a place where even your phone can't find you. You want to be able to talk to God in the way that's comfortable to you, at a volume that's comfortable to you. You can't do that if you're worried about disturbing others. And you want a place quiet enough to be able to sense God's promptings after you stop talking and start listening in your prayer.

In addition to prayer, Bible study and journaling are two real difference-makers that are perfect for quiet times in seclusion with God. What you choose to read in God's Word is up to you. You may choose to study a particular book of the Bible. Or you may want to focus on a specific topic, such as forgiveness or relationships. You may choose to do a read-through-the-Bible-in-a-year program, which is great, as long as you don't race through the passages just so you can get through them. Remember, your goal is to connect with the Lord, not finish an assignment or complete a to-do list.

Study Bibles are invaluable in helping you understand what you read. As you read, think about things you can offer praise or thanksgiving for in your prayers.

You'll also find it helpful to keep a journal open in front of you during your quiet time with God. Write down the things He brings to your mind as you study and pray. Jot down your prayer requests and the answers you receive to those requests so that you can keep track of the Lord's work in your life.

Amazing things can happen when it's just you and God in a quiet, secluded place.

> **HEAVENLY FATHER, THANK YOU FOR THE INCREDIBLE PRIVILEGE I HAVE TO SPEND TIME ALONE WITH YOU ANY TIME I WANT. LET ME NEVER LOSE SIGHT OF YOUR GRACIOUS WILLINGNESS TO MEET ME WHEREVER I CALL OUT TO YOU. GIVE ME THE WISDOM AND DISCERNMENT TO FIND JUST THE RIGHT PLACE TO MAXIMIZE MY QUIET TIME WITH YOU. IN JESUS' NAME. AMEN.**

THE ART OF SPEAKING YOUR MIND

*If you aren't going to say exactly how and what you
feel, you might as well not say anything at all.*

—JOHNNY CASH

Righteous lips are the delight of kings, and one who speaks right is loved.

—PROVERBS 16:13 NASB

Contrary to what some people believe, the First Amendment to the United States Constitution does not guarantee absolute freedom of speech. For example, obscenity isn't protected by the First Amendment. Neither are libel, slander, perjury, blackmail, or fighting words. Like it or not, there are certain parameters that guide our speech.

The same principle applies to believers who desire to express themselves, as Johnny Cash explained. We aren't free to say whatever pops into our heads, heedless of the consequences. The Bible provides some necessary parameters to guide our speech so that our words will bless, instead of curse, the people around us.

"Whoever walks in integrity walks securely, but whoever takes crooked paths will be found out" (Proverbs 10:9 NIV). Integrity is the starting point for expressing ourselves. Our desire to say exactly how and what we feel must be sincere. Our motives must be pure. Before we allow our words to proceed from our mouths, we need to check and recheck them for traces of meanness, revenge, pettiness, sarcasm, or jealousy. Keep in mind that our objective is to strengthen our bond with the people who hear our words.

The apostle Paul wrote, "Be angry, and yet do not sin; do not let the sun go down on your anger" (Ephesians 4:26 NASB). Notice that Paul didn't say, "Do not be angry." Anger is a legitimate emotion. So are sadness and excitement and fear. They're all deserving of expression. But there's a caveat. In expressing them, we can't cross the line of sin. We must be aware of their damaging potential and use caution when we communicate our emotions, especially when they're raw.

"Speaking the truth in love, we are to grow up in all aspects into Him who is the head, that is, Christ" (Ephesians 4:15 NASB). Here's the balancing act we have to pull off. When we communicate truth, our motive must be love. If the person we're talking to can't recognize the love at the root of our speech, we need to try again—and again, until the love is apparent.

"Don't use foul or abusive language. Let everything you say be good and helpful, so that your words will be an encouragement to those who hear them" (Ephesians 4:29 NLT). Here we get a glimpse of the tongue's potential to do extraordinary good. The ability to encourage other people is one of the most powerful gifts God has given us. Under the best of circumstances, words that encourage are a welcome boost—something that can make a person's day. Under the worst of circumstances, words that encourage may be a lifesaver—something that makes a profound difference at just the right time.

God may not always make us aware of the positive impact our words have. But we should always be aware of their potential to do good. If we express the truth from a base of integrity, being careful not to sin in the heat of our emotions, speaking the truth in a loving way, the result will be words of encouragement to others. Everybody wins.

> HEAVENLY FATHER, THANK YOU FOR SHOWING ME IN YOUR WORD HOW TO HONOR YOU WITH MY WORDS. GIVE ME THE AWARENESS TO THINK BEFORE I SPEAK, TO ASK MYSELF WHETHER I'M SPEAKING THE TRUTH IN LOVE. HELP ME LEARN TO USE MY TONGUE TO ENCOURAGE OTHERS INSTEAD OF TEARING THEM DOWN. IN JESUS' NAME. AMEN.

HAPPINESS IS

Happiness is being at peace, being with loved ones, being comfortable . . . but most of all, it's having those loved ones.
—Johnny Cash

A house is built by wisdom and becomes strong through good sense. Through knowledge its rooms are filled with all sorts of precious riches and valuables.
—Proverbs 24:3–4 NLT

Johnny Cash identifies three key ingredients to happiness in the home. The first is peace. Peace is important to God. The apostle Paul showed us God's lofty expectations in this area when he wrote, "Do all that you can to live in peace with everyone" (Romans 12:18 NLT). Peace doesn't always come naturally. For one thing, it usually requires compromise. Sometimes it must be worked out in the aftermath of battle. And that can be a tall order, especially if stubbornness or hard feelings linger. But the rewards of working toward peace are always worth the effort.

Ultimately, peace comes from God. "Then you will experience God's peace, which exceeds anything we can understand. His peace will guard your hearts and minds as you live in Christ Jesus" (Philippians 4:7 NLT). In the home, genuine peace comes from submitting to God and then submitting to one another, with all sides prioritizing the good of the whole family over individual needs and desires. When God's peace dominates, the home becomes a haven.

The second ingredient is comfort. But Johnny Cash was talking about something deeper than creature comforts—a fireplace, a recliner, a king-size bed, cozy blankets scattered around. The comfort he talked about is the sense of feeling *at* home *in* your home. Comfort is knowing that you're surrounded by people who may not always understand you but who genuinely care about you. Comfort is knowing that while you may occasionally face discipline and correction, you won't be judged for mistakes. Comfort is knowing that you have leeway and understanding.

Comfort is knowing that God is at the center of your home—that you're not ultimately responsible for your family's safety and well-being. Comfort is knowing that God cares even more deeply for your loved ones than you do—that He knows exactly what's best for them and how to bring it about.

The third and most important ingredient are our loved ones. One surefire way to foster happiness in our homes is to make sure our loved ones know how much we love them. When we take the time to listen and observe to find out what makes each member of the family feel valued and loved, we can show them our love through more than just words. Our intentional acts of kindness can go a long way to convince someone that they are truly loved and accepted.

Finally, one of the most meaningful ways to show the depth of our love is to pray for our loved ones every day. We can lift them up individually to God as we name the requests we know of in their lives and commit the rest to Him.

As Johnny Cash makes clear, we don't need all three ingredients to be truly happy. As long as we have people who love us and want the best for us, we can find happiness in whatever life throws our way.

> HEAVENLY FATHER, THANK YOU FOR THE PEACE THAT YOU MAKE POSSIBLE, REGARDLESS OF THE CIRCUMSTANCES. THANK YOU FOR THE COMFORT THAT COMES FROM KNOWING MY FUTURE RESTS IN YOUR HANDS. AND THANK YOU FOR THE LOVED ONES YOU'VE ENTRUSTED TO MY CARE. LET ME NEVER TAKE FOR GRANTED THE HAPPINESS THAT YOU MAKE POSSIBLE. IN JESUS' NAME. AMEN.

LIVE YOUR FAITH

Dear Friend,

This book was prayerfully crafted with you, the reader, in mind. Every word, every sentence, every page was thoughtfully written, designed, and packaged to encourage you—right where you are this very moment. At DaySpring, our vision is to see every person experience the life-changing message of God's love. So, as we worked through rough drafts, design changes, edits, and details, we prayed for you to deeply experience His unfailing love, indescribable peace, and pure joy. It is our sincere hope that through these Truth-filled pages your heart will be blessed, knowing that God cares about you—your desires and disappointments, your challenges and dreams.

He knows. He cares. He loves you unconditionally.

BLESSINGS!
THE DAYSPRING BOOK TEAM

Additional copies of this book and
other DaySpring titles can be purchased
at fine retailers everywhere.
Order online at <u>dayspring.com</u>
or
by phone at 1-877-751-4347

JOHNNY CASH

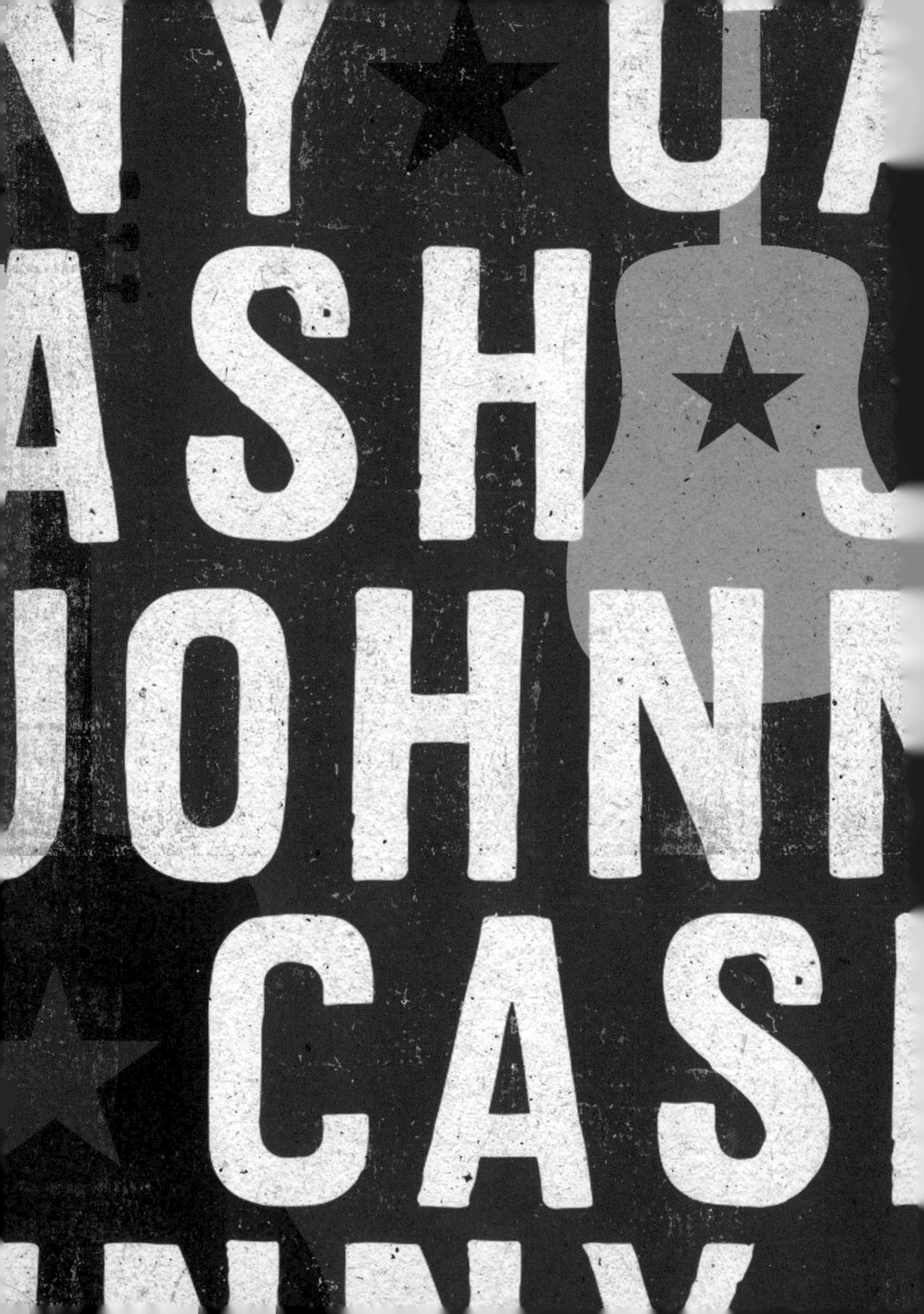